'TIS THE SEASON

'TIS THE SEASON

OVER 100 KID-FRIENDLY COOKIES, BARS, AND CANDIES
TO MAKE THROUGHOUT ALL THE HOLIDAYS

©2016 Time Inc. Books
Published by Oxmoor House,
an imprint of Time Inc. Books
225 Liberty Street, New York, NY 10281

Editor: Meredith L. Butcher

Editorial Assistant: Nicole Fisher

Project Editor: Lacie Pinyan

Senior Designer: Teresa Cole

Junior Designer: AnnaMaria Jacob

Photographers: Iain Bagwell,
Becky Luigart-Stayner

Prop Stylists: Kay E. Clarke,
Mindi Shapiro Levine

Food Stylists: Victoria E. Cox,
Margaret Monroe Dickey,
Catherine Crowell Steele

Recipe Developers and Testers: Julia Levy,
Callie Nash, Karen Rankin

Assistant Production Manager:
Diane Rose Keener

Assistant Production Director:
Sue Chodakiewicz

Copy Editors: Jacqueline Giovanelli,
Susan Kemp

Proofreaders: Lucia Carruthers,
Norma Butterworth-McKittrick

Indexer: Carol Roberts

Fellows: Audrey Davis, Rishon Hanners,
Olivia Pierce, Natalie Schumann,
Mallory Short

This exclusive edition was printed for Kohl's
Department Stores, Inc. (for distribution on
behalf of Kohl's Cares, LLC, its wholly owned
subsidiary) by Time Inc. Books.

Style number 978-0-8487-5180-7
Factory Number 123387
July 2016

ISBN-13: 978-0-8487-5180-7
ISBN-10: 0-8487-5180-9

Library of Congress Control Number:
2016936827

First Edition 2016

Printed in China

10 9 8 7 6 5 4 3 2 1

Time Inc. Books products may be
purchased for business or promotional use.
For information on bulk purchases, please
contact Christi Crowley in the Special Sales
Department at (845) 895-9858.

**We welcome your comments and
suggestions about Time Inc. Books.**

Please write to us at:
Time Inc. Books
Attention: Book Editors
P.O. Box 62310
Tampa, Florida 33662-2310

CONTENTS

GET KIDS INVOLVED

Kids are eager to learn and to get involved with cooking, and everyday tasks such as grocery shopping that may seem mundane to parents can be great learning opportunities. Here are eight easy ways to teach kids about food and nutrition and to encourage healthy lifestyle habits.

GET COOKING.

Involve your child in the cooking process. Though it does require a little patience and time, cooking with your child offers many opportunities to learn and to bond, as well as to establish a lifelong interest in food and nutrition.

TALK ABOUT PORTIONS.

Spending time in the kitchen with your children provides an opportunity to talk to them about how often and how much to eat of their favorite desserts. Don't label desserts as "bad." Instead, discuss how they are treats to be enjoyed on special occasions.

GUIDELINES FOR COOKING WITH KIDS

CLEAN
- Always wash hands before starting to cook.
- Clean up as you cook, making it part of the process.
- Don't mix raw and cooked foods.
- Clean cutting boards and counters that raw meat, poultry, or seafood has touched. It's also helpful to have cutting boards with different colors to identify one for meat and one for fruits and vegetables.

PREPARE
- Set kitchen rules, and communicate those clearly. Read each recipe before beginning, and have your child read it if he or she is able.
- Locate ingredients and equipment, and chop or measure as needed before starting.
- Create a small, safe workplace in the kitchen for younger children, and provide plenty of kid-friendly utensils.

DON'T ASSUME
- Never assume children will know what to do by watching—explain as you go, demonstrate, and then let them try.
- Kids don't necessarily know that an object or utensil may be hot or sharp, so make sure to tell them and to set rules about usage.

PREVENT
- Keep sharp or dangerous items, such as knives, scissors, and food processors, out of reach.
- Clean up spills as they happen.
- Don't sample food until it's done.

SUPERVISE
- Always supervise children in the kitchen.
- For older children, identify what is and isn't OK to do when you're not in the kitchen.

WHY COOK WITH KIDS?
The benefits of cooking with your child include:

- Increased self-confidence for your child
- Practice working as a team
- Development of fine motor skills
- Practice counting and identifying colors
- Greater likelihood your child will try the foods prepared
- Better understanding of nutrition
- Practice with reading and comprehension

PUMPKIN PIE CUTOUT COOKIES, PAGE 12

FALL TREATS

COZY UP WITH THESE
WARM AND TOASTY TREATS!

PUMPKIN PIE CUTOUT COOKIES

Hands-on: 50 minutes
Total: 5 hours, 5 minutes
Makes: about 5 dozen cookies

Cookies:
- 6 ounces (¾ cup) butter, softened
- ¾ cup granulated sugar
- 1 large egg
- 1 teaspoon vanilla extract
- 1¾ cups plus 2 tablespoons (7.9 ounces) all-purpose flour
- 1¾ teaspoons pumpkin pie spice
- ¼ teaspoon salt

Parchment paper

Icing:
- 1 (16-ounce) package powdered sugar
- 2 large pasteurized egg whites
- 2 teaspoons water

Food coloring (optional)

1. Make the cookies: Put the butter and granulated sugar in a large bowl. Beat with an electric mixer at medium speed 5 to 7 minutes or until light and fluffy. Add the egg and vanilla; beat 1 minute.

2. Sift together the flour, pumpkin pie spice, and salt in a bowl. Add to the butter mixture all at once, and beat at medium speed 1 minute or until combined. Flatten the dough into a 1-inch-thick disk, and wrap in plastic wrap. Chill 2 hours.

3. Preheat the oven to 375°F, with the oven racks in the 2 middle positions. Line baking sheets with the parchment paper. Place the dough on a lightly floured surface; roll to ¼-inch thickness. (If the dough gets too soft to handle, chill 5 to 10 minutes.)

4. Cut the dough with desired cutters, and place ½ inch apart on the prepared baking sheets. Reroll the scraps as needed. Chill the cut cookies 30 minutes.

5. Bake at 375°F, 2 sheets at a time, for 9 minutes. Rotate the pans front to back, and top rack to bottom rack. Bake 2 to 4 more minutes or until slightly golden around the edges. Transfer to wire racks, and cool completely (about 15 minutes).

6. Meanwhile, make the icing: Put the powdered sugar, egg whites, and 2 teaspoons water in a bowl. Beat at low speed 2 minutes. (If necessary, add up to 1 tablespoon water, 1 teaspoon at a time, to reach desired consistency.) Divide the icing, and tint with the food coloring, if desired. Cover the icing with plastic wrap or a damp towel when not in use.

7. Spread a thin layer of icing over each cookie. For a swirled effect, immediately dot the cookie with another color of icing, and blend with a wooden pick. Let the base layer of icing dry 10 minutes before piping the details. Let the finished cookies dry 15 minutes before serving.

MOLASSES SPICE CRINKLES

HANDS-ON: 45 minutes
TOTAL: 1 hour, 45 minutes
MAKES: 3 dozen cookies

- 2 cups (9 ounces) all-purpose flour
- 1 teaspoon baking powder
- 1 teaspoon baking soda
- 1 teaspoon ground ginger
- 1 teaspoon ground cinnamon
- ½ teaspoon ground nutmeg
- ¼ teaspoon salt
- ¼ teaspoon ground cloves
- ¼ teaspoon ground allspice
- ¾ cup shortening
- 1 cup granulated sugar
- 1 large egg
- ¼ cup molasses
- 1 cup coarse white sparkling sugar

1. Stir together the flour, baking powder, baking soda, ginger, cinnamon, nutmeg, salt, cloves, and allspice in a medium bowl.

2. Put the shortening in a large bowl. Beat with an electric mixer at medium speed until fluffy. Gradually add the granulated sugar, beating well. Add the egg and molasses; beat well. Gradually add the flour mixture, beating at low speed until blended. Cover; chill 1 hour.

3. Preheat the oven to 375°F. Put the sparkling sugar in a small bowl. Shape the dough into 36 (1-inch) balls; roll in the sparkling sugar. Place the balls 2 inches apart on ungreased baking sheets.

4. Bake at 375°F for 9 to 11 minutes (tops will crack) or just until set. Transfer to wire racks.

FROSTED PUMPKIN COOKIES

HANDS-ON: 1 hour, 10 minutes
TOTAL: 2 hours
MAKES: 30 cookies

Cookies:
- ⅔ cup granulated sugar
- ⅔ cup packed brown sugar
- 6 ounces (¾ cup) butter or margarine, softened
- 1 teaspoon vanilla extract
- ½ cup canned pumpkin (not pumpkin pie mix)
- 2 large eggs
- 2¼ cups (10.1 ounces) all-purpose flour
- 1 teaspoon baking soda
- 1 teaspoon ground cinnamon
- ½ teaspoon salt

Browned Butter Frosting:
- 3 cups powdered sugar
- 1 teaspoon vanilla extract
- 3 to 4 tablespoons milk
- 3 ounces (⅓ cup) butter (do not use margarine or spread)

1. **Make the cookies:** Preheat the oven to 375°F. Put the granulated sugar, brown sugar, ¾ cup butter, and 1 teaspoon vanilla in a large bowl. Beat with an electric mixer at medium speed, scraping bowl occasionally, until well blended. Beat in the pumpkin and eggs until well mixed. Beat in the flour, baking soda, cinnamon, and salt at low speed.

2. Drop the dough by heaping tablespoonfuls onto ungreased baking sheets. Bake at 375°F for 10 to 12 minutes or until almost no indentation remains when touched in the center. Immediately transfer to wire racks. Cool completely (about 45 minutes).

3. **Make the frosting:** Stir together the powdered sugar, 1 teaspoon vanilla, and 3 tablespoons milk in a medium bowl. Put ⅓ cup butter in a 1-quart saucepan. Heat over medium, stirring constantly, just until light brown. Pour the browned butter over the powdered sugar mixture. Beat at low speed about 1 minute or until smooth. Gradually beat in just enough of the remaining 1 tablespoon milk until the frosting is creamy and spreadable. Generously frost the cookies.

OATMEAL-PEAR-TOFFEE COOKIES

HANDS-ON: 35 minutes
TOTAL: 35 minutes
MAKES: 2 dozen cookies

Cooking spray

- 1 (17.5-ounce) pouch oatmeal cookie mix
- 3 ounces (⅓ cup) butter, softened
- 1 large egg
- ¼ teaspoon ground nutmeg
- ¾ cup finely chopped peeled pear
- ⅔ cup toffee bits

1. Preheat the oven to 350°F. Coat a baking sheet with cooking spray.

2. Stir together the cookie mix, butter, egg, and nutmeg in a medium bowl until blended. Stir in the pear and toffee bits. Shape the dough into 24 (1-inch) balls. Place the balls 2 inches apart on the prepared baking sheet.

3. Bake 350°F for 14 to 16 minutes or until golden brown. Cool 5 minutes. Transfer to a wire rack.

Make
For extra toffee flavor, drizzle these cookies with toffee or caramel sundae syrup.

NUTTY CHOCOLATE THUMBPRINTS

- -

HANDS-ON: 40 minutes
TOTAL: 1 hour, 30 minutes
MAKES: 30 cookies

Cookies:

Parchment paper

1⅔ cups (7.5 ounces) all-purpose flour

⅔ cup unsweetened cocoa

½ teaspoon baking powder

½ teaspoon salt

4 ounces (½ cup) butter, softened

1 cup firmly packed light brown sugar

¾ cup powdered sugar

¾ cup creamy peanut butter

2 large eggs

1 teaspoon vanilla extract

Filling:

¼ cup creamy peanut butter

2 tablespoons butter, softened

2 ounces bittersweet chocolate (60% cocoa), chopped

1½ cups powdered sugar

2 to 3 tablespoons milk, at room temperature

1. Make the cookies: Preheat the oven to 350°F. Line a baking sheet with the parchment paper. Whisk together the first 4 ingredients. Put ½ cup butter in a large bowl. Beat with an electric mixer at medium-high speed until fluffy. Add the brown sugar and powdered sugar; beat until well blended. Beat in the peanut butter. Add the eggs, 1 at a time, beating until blended. Beat in the vanilla. Reduce speed to medium-low, and gradually add the flour mixture, beating just until blended.

2. Shape the dough into 30 balls. Place 12 balls 2 inches apart on the prepared baking sheet. Press your thumb into each ball, forming an indentation. Bake at 350°F for 12 minutes or until set; cool 5 minutes. Transfer the cookies to a wire rack. Repeat with remaining dough.

3. Make the filling: Put the peanut butter and butter in a large bowl. Beat at medium speed until smooth. Put the chopped chocolate in a microwave-safe bowl. Microwave at HIGH 1 to 2 minutes or until smooth, stirring every 30 seconds. Add the melted chocolate to the peanut butter mixture, and beat at medium speed just until blended. Gradually add 1½ cups powdered sugar to the peanut butter mixture alternately with 2 tablespoons milk, beginning with the sugar. Beat at low speed just until blended after each addition. Beat in up to 1 tablespoon milk, 1 teaspoon. at a time, until desired consistency is reached. Spoon the filling into a zip-top plastic bag; snip 1 corner of the bag to make a small hole, and pipe the filling into the center of each cookie.

GERMAN CHOCOLATE-PECAN PIE BARS

HANDS-ON: 20 minutes
TOTAL: 3 hours, 40 minutes
MAKES: 2 dozen bars

 3 cups pecan halves and pieces
Heavy-duty aluminum foil
 1¾ cups (7.9 ounces) all-purpose flour
 ¾ cup powdered sugar
 6 ounces (¾ cup) cold butter, cubed
 ¼ cup unsweetened cocoa
 1½ cups semisweet chocolate chips
 ¾ cup firmly packed brown sugar
 ¾ cup light corn syrup
 2 ounces (¼ cup) butter, melted
 3 large eggs, lightly beaten
 1 cup flaked sweetened coconut

1. Preheat the oven to 350°F. Put the pecans in a single layer in a shallow pan. Bake for 8 to 10 minutes or until lightly toasted and fragrant, stirring halfway through.

2. Line the bottom and sides of a 13- x 9-inch pan with heavy-duty aluminum foil, allowing 2 to 3 inches to extend over sides. Lightly grease the foil.

3. Put the flour and next 3 ingredients in a food processor; pulse 5 to 6 times or until the mixture resembles coarse meal. Press the mixture into the bottom and ¾ inch up the sides of the prepared pan.

4. Bake the crust at 350°F for 15 minutes. Remove from the oven, and sprinkle the chocolate chips over the crust. Cool completely on a wire rack (about 30 minutes).

5. Whisk together the brown sugar and next 3 ingredients until smooth. Stir in the coconut and toasted pecans, and spoon into the prepared crust.

6. Bake at 350°F for 25 to 30 minutes or until golden and set. Cool completely on a wire rack (about 1 hour). Chill 1 hour. Lift the baked bars from the pan, using the foil sides as handles. Transfer to a cutting board. Gently remove the foil; cut into 6 rows by 4 rows.

PECAN PIE BARS

HANDS-ON: 20 minutes
TOTAL: 3 hours, 25 minutes
MAKES: 2 dozen bars

Crust:
- 2½ cups (11.25 ounces) all-purpose flour
- ⅔ cup powdered sugar
- ¾ cup chopped toasted pecans
- ½ teaspoon kosher salt
- 8 ounces (1 cup) butter, cubed
- Heavy-duty aluminum foil
- Vegetable cooking spray

Filling:
- ¾ cup cane syrup
- ½ cup firmly packed dark brown sugar
- 6 tablespoons heavy cream
- 6 ounces (¾ cup) cold butter
- ¼ teaspoon kosher salt
- 1 teaspoon vanilla extract
- 3 cups coarsely chopped toasted pecans

1. Make the crust: Preheat the oven to 350°F. Pulse the flour and next 3 ingredients in a food processor 8 to 10 times or until thoroughly combined and pecans are finely chopped; add butter, and pulse 8 or 9 times or until mixture resembles coarse meal. Line bottom and sides of a 13- x 9-inch pan with aluminum foil, allowing 2 to 3 inches to extend over sides; lightly grease foil with cooking spray. Press the crust mixture into the bottom of a prepared pan.

2. Bake at 350°F for 20 to 25 minutes or until lightly browned. Cool completely on a wire rack (about 25 minutes).

3. Make the filling: Bring syrup and next 4 ingredients to a boil in a large saucepan over medium heat, stirring constantly until butter melts and mixture is smooth; boil, stirring constantly, 1 minute. Remove from heat, and stir in vanilla and 3 cups coarsely chopped toasted pecans. Pour hot filling over cooled crust.

4. Bake at 350°F for 14 to 16 minutes or until the filling bubbles in the center. Cool completely in the pan on a wire rack (about 1 hour). Chill 1 hour. Lift the bars from the pan, using the foil sides as handles. Gently remove the foil; cut into 6 rows by 4 rows.

S'MORES BARS

HANDS-ON: 10 minutes
TOTAL: 1 hour, 45 minutes
MAKES: 18 bars

Heavy-duty aluminum foil

Cooking spray

6 graham cracker rectangles

2 (16-ounce) packages refrigerated chocolate chip cookies

4 (1.55-ounce) bars milk chocolate candy, separated into pieces

3 cups miniature marshmallows

1. Preheat the oven to 350°F. Line a 9-inch square pan with aluminum foil, leaving 1 inch of the foil overhanging on 2 opposite sides of the pan; coat the foil with cooking spray.

2. Arrange the graham crackers in the bottom of the pan, breaking to fit as needed. Press 32 of the cookies in an even layer on the crackers. Sprinkle the chocolate candy pieces over the cookies. Crumble the remaining 16 cookies into small pieces; sprinkle over the chocolate layer.

3. Bake at 350°F for 30 to 35 minutes or just until set.

4. Set the oven to broil. Sprinkle the marshmallows over the bars. Broil 30 seconds or until the marshmallows are golden brown. Cool in the pan on a wire rack (1 hour). Lift the bars from the pan, using the foil sides as handles. Cut into 6 rows by 3 rows. Store tightly covered at room temperature.

MAKE
For best results, use a lightly greased chef's knife to cut the bars.

ROOT BEER FLOAT BROWNIES

HANDS-ON: 15 minutes
TOTAL: 2 hours, 5 minutes
MAKES: 16 brownies

Cooking spray

- 1⅓ cups (10.5 ounces) all-purpose flour
- 2 cups granulated sugar
- ¾ cup unsweetened Dutch-process cocoa
- ½ teaspoon salt
- 8 ounces (1 cup) butter, cut into pieces
- ½ cup semisweet chocolate chips
- 4 large eggs
- ½ teaspoon root beer extract
- ½ cup powdered sugar
- 2 tablespoons root beer

1. Preheat the oven to 325°F. Coat an 8-inch square pan with cooking spray.

2. Stir together the flour, the sugar, ½ cup of the cocoa, and the salt in a medium bowl.

3. Put the butter and chocolate chips in a large microwave-safe bowl. Microwave, uncovered, at HIGH 2 minutes, stirring after 1 minute, until melted and mixture can be stirred smooth. Stir in the flour mixture, eggs, and root beer extract. Pour the batter into the prepared pan.

4. Bake at 325°F for 50 minutes or until a wooden pick inserted into the center comes out almost clean. Cool completely in the pan on a wire rack (about 1 hour).

5. Stir together the powdered sugar, the remaining ¼ cup cocoa, and the root beer in a small bowl with whisk until smooth. Pour the glaze over the brownies. Cut into 4 rows by 4 rows.

PUMPKIN-CHOCOLATE BROWNIES

HANDS-ON: 40 minutes
TOTAL: 4 hours, 5 minutes
MAKES: 2 dozen brownies

Butter

Parchment paper

1¼ cups semisweet chocolate chips

8 ounces (1 cup) unsalted butter, cut into pieces

3 ounces unsweetened chocolate, chopped

6 large eggs

1 cup plus 2 tablespoons granulated sugar

2 tablespoons cold brewed coffee

1 tablespoon vanilla extract

⅔ cup (3 ounces) all-purpose flour

1½ teaspoons baking powder

1 teaspoon kosher salt

1 (15-ounce) can pumpkin (not pumpkin pie mix)

½ cup heavy cream

⅓ cup firmly packed light brown sugar

1½ teaspoons pumpkin pie spice

1. Preheat the oven to 350°F. Grease a 13- x 9-inch baking pan with butter. Line the bottom and sides of the pan with the parchment paper, allowing 2 to 3 inches to extend over the sides. Grease with the butter, and flour the parchment paper.

2. Pour water to a depth of 1 inch in the bottom of a double boiler over medium heat; bring to a boil. Reduce heat, and simmer. Put the chocolate chips, unsalted butter, and unsweetened chocolate in the top of a double boiler over the simmering water. Cook, stirring occasionally, 5 to 6 minutes or until melted. Remove from heat; cool 10 minutes.

3. Whisk together 3 of the eggs, the granulated sugar, the coffee, and the vanilla in a large bowl. Gradually whisk the warm chocolate mixture into the egg mixture; cool 10 minutes.

4. Sift together the flour, baking powder, and ½ teaspoon of the salt in a bowl. Whisk into the chocolate mixture. Pour the batter into the prepared pan, reserving ⅔ cup.

5. Whisk together the pumpkin, the next 3 ingredients, the remaining 3 eggs, and the remaining ½ teaspoon salt; pour over the brownie batter in the pan. Top with the reserved brownie batter, and swirl the batter gently 3 times in 1 direction and 3 times in the opposite direction with a knife or the end of a wooden spoon.

6. Bake at 350°F for 45 to 50 minutes or until a wooden pick inserted into the center comes out with a few moist crumbs. Cool completely on a wire rack (about 2 hours). Lift the brownies from the pan, using the parchment paper sides as handles. Gently remove the parchment paper, and cut the brownies into 6 rows by 4 rows.

BUTTERSCOTCH BLONDIES

HANDS-ON: 12 minutes
TOTAL: 52 minutes
MAKES: 16 blondies

- 1 cup (4.5 ounces) whole-wheat pastry flour
- 1/2 teaspoon baking powder
- 1/2 teaspoon salt
- 1/4 cup butterscotch chips
- 2 tablespoons half-and-half
- 3/4 cup packed brown sugar
- 3 tablespoons canola oil
- 3 tablespoons butter, melted
- 1 teaspoon vanilla extract
- 2 large eggs
- 1/3 cup semisweet chocolate chips
- **Cooking spray**

TIP: Even though whole-wheat pastry flour is more finely ground than regular whole-wheat flour, you may use regular as a substitute.

1. Preheat the oven to 350°F.

2. Stir together flour, baking powder, and salt in a medium bowl with a whisk until thoroughly combined.

3. Put the butterscotch chips and half-and-half in a medium microwave-safe bowl; microwave at HIGH 45 seconds, stirring at 15-second intervals. Stir until smooth. Add the brown sugar, canola oil, butter, vanilla, and eggs, and beat with an electric mixer at high speed 2 minutes. Add the flour mixture to the butterscotch mixture, stirring just until combined. Stir in the chocolate chips.

4. Pour batter into an 8-inch square metal baking pan coated with cooking spray. Bake at 350°F for 40 minutes or until a wooden pick inserted into center comes out with a few moist crumbs. Cool in the pan on a wire rack.

BUCKEYE BROWNIES

HANDS-ON: 20 minutes
TOTAL: 1 hour, 10 minutes
MAKES: 32 brownies

- 1 (18.3-ounce) package fudge brownie mix

Water, vegetable oil, and eggs called for on brownie mix package

- 1 cup creamy peanut butter
- 4 ounces (½ cup) butter, softened (do not use margarine)
- 2 cups powdered sugar
- 2 tablespoons milk
- 1 (1-pound) container chocolate creamy ready-to-spread frosting

1. Preheat the oven to 350°F (325°F for a dark or nonstick pan). Make and bake brownies as directed on box for a 13- x 9-inch pan, using water, oil, and eggs. (Do not overbake.) Cool completely in the pan on a wire rack (about 45 minutes).

2. Put the peanut butter and butter in a large bowl. Beat with an electric mixer at medium speed until smooth. Gradually beat in the powdered sugar and milk until well blended. Beat at medium speed until creamy. Spread evenly over brownies.

3. Put the frosting in a small microwave-safe bowl; microwave at HIGH 25 seconds; stir until smooth. Spread frosting evenly over the peanut butter layer. Chill 2 hours or until the frosting is set. Cut into 8 rows by 4 rows. Store covered in refrigerator.

LOADED BLONDIE BARS

HANDS-ON: 10 minutes
TOTAL: 2 hours
MAKES: 3 dozen bars

- 20 thin chocolate wafer cookies, crushed (about 1¼ cups)
- 3 tablespoons butter, melted

Cooking spray

- 1⅓ cups packed brown sugar
- 5 ounces (⅔ cup) butter, softened
- 1 teaspoon vanilla extract
- 2 large eggs
- 1 cup (4.5 ounces) all-purpose flour
- ¼ teaspoon salt
- 2 (1.4-ounce) bars chocolate-covered English toffee candy, chopped
- 1 cup chopped pecans
- 1½ cups semisweet chocolate morsels

1. Preheat the oven to 350°F. Stir together the crushed cookies and melted butter. Press the mixture into the bottom of a 9-inch square pan coated with cooking spray.

2. Put the brown sugar and ⅔ cup butter in a large bowl. Beat with an electric mixer at medium speed until light and fluffy. Beat in vanilla and eggs until blended. Gradually add the flour and salt, beating at low speed just until blended. Stir in the toffee candy, pecans, and chocolate morsels. Spread over crust.

3. Bake 350°F for 50 to 55 minutes or until set. Cool completely in the pan on a wire rack. Cut into 6 rows by 6 rows.

CHERRY CHEESECAKE BROWNIES

Hands-On: 34 minutes
Total: 1 hour, 24 minutes
Makes: 20 brownies

Cheesecake:
- ½ cup chopped dried tart cherries
- 1 tablespoon cherry liqueur
- ¼ cup granulated sugar
- 6 ounces ⅓-less-fat cream cheese
- 1 tablespoon matzo cake meal
- ¼ teaspoon vanilla extract
- 1 large egg, lightly beaten

Brownies:
Cooking spray
- 1½ teaspoons unsweetened cocoa
- 3 ounces bittersweet chocolate, finely chopped
- 1 ounce unsweetened chocolate, finely chopped
- 3 ounces (⅓ cup) butter, cut into small pieces
- ½ teaspoon vanilla extract
- 2 large egg whites
- 1 large egg
- ¾ cup (3.4 ounces) all-purpose flour
- ¾ cup granulated sugar
- ½ teaspoon baking powder
- ⅛ teaspoon salt

1. Preheat the oven to 325°F.

2. Make the cheesecake: Put the cherries and liqueur in a microwave-safe bowl. Microwave at HIGH 45 seconds or until boiling; let stand 20 minutes. Put ¼ cup sugar and cream cheese in a large bowl. Beat with an electric mixer at medium speed 1 minute or until smooth. Add the matzo meal, ¼ teaspoon vanilla, and 1 egg; beat just until blended. Stir in cherry mixture.

3. Make the brownies: Coat a 9-inch square metal baking pan with cooking spray; dust with the cocoa. Put the chocolates and butter in a microwave-safe dish; microwave at HIGH 1 minute, stirring every 20 seconds. Let stand 5 minutes. Stir in ½ teaspoon vanilla, egg whites, and 1 egg. Stir together the flour, ¾ cup sugar, baking powder, and salt in a large bowl. Stir chocolate mixture into flour mixture.

4. Scrape half of the brownie batter into prepared pan. Dot the top with half of the cheesecake batter. Top with the remaining brownie batter. Dot with the remaining cheesecake batter. Swirl the batters using the tip of a knife. Bake at 325°F for 50 minutes or until a wooden pick inserted into the center comes out with a few moist crumbs. Cool completely in the pan on a wire rack. Cut into 4 rows by 5 rows.

PUMPKIN SWIRL BLONDIES

HANDS-ON: 15 minutes
TOTAL: 1 hour, 55 minutes
MAKES: 2 dozen bars

Shortening or cooking spray

- 8 ounces (1 cup) butter or margarine, melted
- 2 cups packed brown sugar
- 1½ teaspoons vanilla extract
- 3 eggs
- 2 cups (9 ounces) all-purpose flour
- 2 teaspoons pumpkin pie spice
- ½ teaspoon baking powder
- ½ teaspoon salt
- 1 (8 ounce) package cream cheese, softened
- ½ cup granulated sugar

1. Preheat the oven to 350°F. Grease a 13- x 9-inch pan with shortening or cooking spray.

2. In a medium bowl, mix the melted butter, brown sugar, 1 teaspoon of the vanilla, and 2 of the eggs with a whisk until well blended. Stir in the flour, pumpkin pie spice, baking powder, and salt until blended. Spread two-thirds of the batter into the prepared pan.

3. Beat the cream cheese, the granulated sugar, and the remaining ½ teaspoon vanilla with an electric mixer at medium speed until smooth. Beat in the remaining egg. Spoon the mixture by tablespoonfuls over the batter in the pan. Spoon the remaining brownie batter over the cream cheese mixture. Swirl the cream cheese mixture through the batter with a knife.

4. Bake at 350°F for 35 to 40 minutes or until a wooden pick inserted into the center comes out clean. Cool completely in the pan on a cooling rack, about 1 hour. Cut into 6 rows by 4 rows.

FRESH APPLE CAKE WITH BROWNED BUTTER FROSTING

HANDS-ON: 25 minutes
TOTAL: 3 hours, 15 minutes
MAKES: 15 servings

1½ cups chopped pecans

Cooking spray

2 cups (9 ounces) all-purpose flour

2 teaspoons ground cinnamon

1 teaspoon baking soda

1 teaspoon salt

4 ounces (½ cup) butter, melted

2 cups sugar

2 large eggs

2 teaspoons vanilla extract

2½ pounds Granny Smith apples (about 4 large), peeled, cut into ¼-inch wedges

8 ounces (1 cup) butter

1 (16-ounce) box powdered sugar

¼ cup milk

1. Preheat the oven to 350°F. Spread the pecans in an ungreased shallow pan. Bake, uncovered, for 6 to 10 minutes, stirring occasionally, until light brown. Cool completely.

2. Coat a 13-x 9-inch pan with cooking spray. Stir together the flour, cinnamon, baking soda, and salt in a medium bowl. Stir together the melted butter, sugar, eggs, and 1 teaspoon of the vanilla in a large bowl until blended. Stir in the flour mixture just until blended. Stir in the apples and 1 cup of the toasted pecans. (The batter will be very thick, similar to cookie dough.) Spread the batter in the prepared pan.

3. Bake at 350°F for 45 minutes or until a wooden pick inserted into the center comes out clean. Cool completely in the pan on a wire rack.

4. Meanwhile, cook 1 cup butter over medium heat 6 to 8 minutes in a 1-quart heavy saucepan, stirring constantly, until the butter begins to turn golden brown. Immediately remove from the heat, and pour into a small bowl. Cover; chill 1 hour or until the butter begins to solidify.

5. Beat the browned butter with an electric mixer at medium speed until fluffy. Gradually add the powdered sugar alternately with the milk, beating at low speed until blended. Stir in the remaining 1 teaspoon vanilla. Frost the cake. Sprinkle with the remaining ½ cup toasted pecans. Cover and store in the refrigerator.

CARAMEL APPLE CIDER CUPCAKES

HANDS-ON: 25 minutes
TOTAL: 1 hour, 25 minutes
MAKES: 2 dozen cupcakes

- 24   paper baking cup liners
- 1   (15.25-ounce) box spice cake mix
- Water, vegetable oil, and eggs called for on cake mix box
- 1   cup chopped peeled apple (1 medium)
- 12   ounces cream cheese, softened
- 8   ounces (1 cup) butter, softened
- 4   cups powdered sugar
- ½   cup caramel topping
- 24   (3-inch) cinnamon sticks
- Ground cinnamon

1. Preheat the oven to 350°F. Line 2 regular-sized muffin pans with paper baking cups.

2. Make the cake mix as directed on the box, using the water, oil, and eggs. Stir in the chopped apple. Divide the batter evenly among the prepared muffin cups.

3. Bake at 350°F for 18 to 20 minutes or until a wooden pick inserted into the center comes out clean. Cool 10 minutes. Transfer to wire racks. Cool completely.

4. Put the cream cheese and butter in a large bowl. Beat with an electric mixer at medium speed until well blended. Beat in the powdered sugar until smooth. Spoon the frosting into a decorating bag fitted with a star tip; pipe on the tops of the cupcakes. Drizzle with the caramel topping. Top each cupcake with 1 cinnamon stick. Sprinkle with the ground cinnamon. Store loosely covered in the refrigerator.

CHOCOLATE CHIP COOKIE BABY CAKES

HANDS-ON: 1 hour, 10 minutes
TOTAL: 3 hours, 15 minutes
MAKES: 3 dozen cakes

Cooking spray
- 1 cup semisweet chocolate chips (6 ounces)
- ½ cup coarsely chopped pecans
- ½ cup packed brown sugar
- ½ teaspoon vanilla extract
- ⅛ teaspoon salt
- 2 large eggs
- 1 (17.5-ounce) package chocolate chip cookie mix
- 4 ounces (½ cup) butter, softened

Powdered sugar

1. Preheat the oven to 350°F. Coat 2 18-cup mini muffin pans with cooking spray.

2. Stir together the chocolate chips, pecans, brown sugar, vanilla, salt, and 1 egg in a medium bowl until blended. Cover and chill.

3. Stir together the cookie mix, the butter, and the remaining egg in a large bowl until a soft dough forms. Shape 36 (1-inch) balls; place in muffin cups. Bake at 350°F for 8 minutes or until edges are set.

4. Spoon chilled chocolate morsel mixture evenly over baby cakes. Bake 8 more minutes. Cool in the pans 5 minutes. Transfer the cupcakes from the pans to wire racks, and cool completely. Sprinkle with powdered sugar.

MAKE
These cute little cakes go perfectly with a cup of bold coffee.

STRIPED PEPPERMINT COOKIES, PAGE 36

COOKIE SWAP

SHARE THESE FESTIVE AND FLAVORFUL COOKIES WITH FRIENDS AND FAMILY!

STRIPED PEPPERMINT COOKIES

HANDS-ON: 20 minutes
TOTAL: 3 hours
MAKES: 64 cookies

Plastic wrap

- 8 ounces (1 cup) butter, softened
- 1 cup granulated sugar
- 1 large egg
- 1/2 teaspoon peppermint extract
- 2 1/4 cups (10.1 ounces) all-purpose flour
- 1/4 teaspoon salt
- 1 teaspoon red food coloring paste

1. Line an 8- x 4-inch loaf pan with plastic wrap, allowing the wrap to extend 1 inch over the sides of the pan. Put the butter and sugar in a large bowl. Beat with an electric mixer at medium speed until light and fluffy. Add the egg and peppermint extract, and beat just until blended. Add the flour and salt, beating at medium-low speed until blended.

2. Divide the dough in half. Tint half of the dough with red food coloring, kneading with gloved hands until well blended. Press half of the plain dough evenly into the bottom of the prepared pan. Gently press half of the red dough evenly over the plain dough. Repeat the layers with the remaining dough. Cover with plastic wrap; chill 2 hours or until firm.

3. Preheat the oven to 350°F. Remove the dough from the loaf pan; unwrap. Cut the dough in half lengthwise. Cut each half crosswise into 1/4-inch-thick slices. Place the slices 2 inches apart on an ungreased baking sheets. Bake at 350°F 10 to 12 minutes or until set. Cool 2 minutes. Transfer to wire racks, and cool completely.

MAKE
Impress your guests by serving this on a three-tiered tower at your next holiday party.

LEMON-GLAZED SPRITZ COOKIES

HANDS-ON: 40 minutes
TOTAL: 1 hour, 32 minutes
MAKES: 9 dozen cookies

8 ounces (1 cup) butter, softened

1 cup granulated sugar

1 large egg

2 teaspoons grated lemon zest

1 teaspoon vanilla extract

2½ cups (11.25 ounces) all-purpose flour

¼ teaspoon salt

Waxed paper

2 cups powdered sugar

¼ cup fresh lemon juice

1. Preheat the oven to 375°F. Put the butter in a large bowl. Beat with an electric mixer at medium speed until creamy; gradually add the granulated sugar, beating until light and fluffy. Add the egg, lemon zest, and vanilla; beat well. Stir together the flour and salt; gradually add to the butter mixture, beating at low speed just until blended.

2. Use a cookie press fitted with a wreath-shaped disk to shape the dough into 1½-inch cookies, following the manufacturer's instructions. Place on ungreased baking sheets.

3. Bake at 375°F for 7 to 9 minutes or until edges are golden brown. Cool on baking sheets 2 minutes. Transfer to wire racks, and cool completely (about 10 minutes).

4. Place the wire racks over a waxed paper-lined surface. Whisk together the powdered sugar and lemon juice in a small bowl until smooth. Dip the tops of the cookies into the glaze, allowing excess to drip back into bowl. Place the cookies, glazed sides up, on wire racks. Let the glaze harden at least 15 minutes.

BLACKBERRY THUMBPRINTS

HANDS-ON: 1 hour, 10 minutes
TOTAL: 2 hours
MAKES: 2 dozen cookies

Parchment paper

- ½ **cup slivered almonds**
- 8 **ounces (1 cup) butter, softened**
- 1 **cup powdered sugar**
- 2 **cups (9 ounces) all-purpose flour**
- ¼ **teaspoon salt**
- ¼ **teaspoon ground cloves**
- ¼ **teaspoon ground cinnamon**
- ½ **cup seedless blackberry preserves**

1. Preheat the oven to 350°F. Line baking sheets with the parchment paper. Spread almonds in an ungreased shallow pan. Bake at 350°F, uncovered, for 6 to 10 minutes, stirring occasionally, until light brown. Cool. Reduce the oven temperature to 325°F.

2. Put the almonds in a blender or food processor, and process 30 seconds or until finely ground.

3. Put the butter into a large bowl. Beat with an electric mixer at medium speed until creamy. Gradually add the powdered sugar, beating well at low speed.

4. Stir together the flour, salt, cloves, cinnamon, and ground almonds; gradually add the flour mixture to the butter mixture, beating at low speed just until the mixture is blended.

5. Shape the dough into 24 (¾-inch) balls. Place the balls 2 inches apart on the prepared baking sheets. Press your thumb into each ball, forming an indentation. Bake at 325°F for 12 to 15 minutes or until the edges are light golden brown. Cool on the baking sheets 2 minutes. Transfer to wire racks, and cool completely (about 20 minutes).

6. Spoon the preserves into a small zip-top plastic freezer bag; seal bag. Cut off a tiny corner of the bag; squeeze the bag to pipe the preserves into the center of each cookie.

TOASTED COCONUT CHOCOLATE CHUNK COOKIES

HANDS-ON: 15 minutes
TOTAL: 32 minutes
MAKES: 25 cookies

Cooking spray

- 1 **cup flaked sweetened coconut**
- 1 **cup (4.5 ounces) all-purpose flour**
- ½ **teaspoon baking powder**
- ¼ **teaspoon baking soda**
- ⅛ **teaspoon salt**
- ¾ **cup packed brown sugar**
- 2 **ounces (¼ cup) unsalted butter, softened**
- 1 **teaspoon vanilla extract**
- 1 **large egg**
- 2 **ounces dark chocolate (70% cacao), chopped**

1. Preheat the oven to 350°F. Coat baking sheets with the cooking spray.

2. Arrange the coconut in a single layer in a small baking pan. Bake at 350° for 7 minutes or until lightly toasted, stirring once. Set aside to cool.

3. Stir together the flour, baking powder, baking soda, and salt in a medium bowl with a whisk until blended. Put the sugar and butter into a large bowl. Beat with an electric mixer at medium speed until well blended. Beat in the vanilla and egg. Add the flour mixture, beating at low speed just until combined. Stir in the toasted coconut and chocolate.

4. Drop dough by level tablespoons 2 inches apart onto prepared baking sheets. Bake at 350°F for 10 minutes or until bottoms of cookies just begin to brown. Transfer to wire racks. Cool completely.

TIP: Watch the coconut like a hawk—it can go from toasty golden to burnt very quickly.

PEANUT BUTTER AND JELLY THUMBPRINTS

HANDS-ON: 15 minutes
TOTAL: 1 hour, 30 minutes
MAKES: 3 dozen cookies

2 cups (9 ounces) all-purpose flour

¼ teaspoon salt

¾ cup packed brown sugar

⅔ cup granulated sugar

½ cup chunky peanut butter

2 ounces (¼ cup) butter, softened

2 large eggs

1 teaspoon vanilla extract

Parchment paper

Cooking spray

7 tablespoons seedless raspberry preserves

1 tablespoon fresh lemon juice

1. Whisk together the flour and salt.

2. Put the sugars, peanut butter, and butter in a large bowl. Beat with an electric mixer at medium speed until well combined. Add the eggs, 1 at a time, beating well after each addition. Beat in the vanilla. Gradually add the flour mixture to the sugar mixture, beating at low speed just until combined.

3. Line baking sheets with the parchment paper. Lightly coat your hands with cooking spray. Shape the dough into 36 balls (about 2½ teaspoons each). Place the balls 2 inches apart on the prepared baking sheets. Press your thumb into the center of each dough ball, leaving an indentation. Cover and chill 1 hour.

4. Preheat the oven to 350°F. Uncover the dough. Bake at 350°F for 14 minutes or until lightly browned. Transfer the cookies to a wire rack. Cool completely.

5. Put the preserves in a small microwave-safe bowl, and microwave at HIGH 20 seconds, stirring once. Add the juice, stirring until smooth. Spoon about ½ teaspoon of the preserves mixture into the center of each cookie.

RASPBERRY THUMBPRINT COOKIES

HANDS-ON: 15 minutes
TOTAL: 25 minutes
MAKES: 3 dozen cookies

Parchment paper

Masking tape

- ¾ cup (3 ounces) grated almond paste
- ⅔ cup granulated sugar
- 2½ ounces (⅓ cup) butter, softened
- ¼ teaspoon vanilla extract
- 1 large egg white
- 1¼ cups (5.6 ounces) all-purpose flour
- ¼ teaspoon salt
- 6 tablespoons raspberry jam

1. Preheat the oven to 325°F.

2. Line 2 large baking sheets with parchment paper; secure to the baking sheets with masking tape.

3. Put the almond paste, sugar, and butter in a bowl. Beat with an electric mixer at medium speed 4 minutes or until light and fluffy. Add the vanilla and egg white; beat well.

4. Stir together the flour and salt. Add to the almond paste mixture; beat at low speed until well blended. Turn the dough out onto a lightly floured surface, and shape the dough into 36 (1-inch) balls. Place the balls 1 inch apart on the prepared baking sheets, and press your thumb into the center of each cookie, leaving an indentation. Bake at 325°F for 10 minutes or until golden.

5. Transfer the cookies to wire racks. Cool. Spoon about ½ teaspoon of the jam into the center of each cookie.

TIP: Almond paste makes the dough moist and pliable. Look for it in the supermarket baking aisle. The large holes of a box grater work well for grating the almond paste.

CANDY BAR SUGAR COOKIES

HANDS-ON: 15 minutes
TOTAL: 47 minutes
MAKES: 4 dozen cookies

Parchment paper
- ½ **cup shortening**
- 2 **ounces (¼ cup) butter, softened**
- ½ **cup firmly packed light brown sugar**
- 1 **large egg**
- 1½ **teaspoons vanilla extract**
- 2 **cups (9 ounces) all-purpose flour**
- 1½ **teaspoons baking powder**
- ½ **teaspoon baking soda**
- ½ **teaspoon salt**
- 2 **(2.1-ounce) chocolate-covered crispy peanut-buttery candy bars, coarsely chopped**
- 6 **tablespoons turbinado sugar**

TIP: For an even more decadent treat, drizzle the cooled cookies with melted chocolate.

1. Preheat the oven to 375°. Line the baking sheets with the parchment paper. Put the shortening and butter into a large bowl. Beat with an electric mixer at medium speed until light and fluffy. Gradually add the brown sugar, beating until smooth. Add the egg and vanilla, beating until blended.

2. Stir together the flour and next 3 ingredients; gradually add to the shortening mixture, beating just until blended. Stir in the candy. Put the turbinado sugar in a small bowl. Shape the dough into 48 (1-inch) balls; roll each ball in turbinado sugar. Place the balls 3 inches apart on the prepared baking sheets.

3. Bake at 375°F for 9 to 10 minutes or until lightly browned. Cool 2 minutes on the baking sheets; transfer to wire racks, and cool completely (about 20 minutes).

CRANBERRY-NUT CHOCOLATE CHIP COOKIES

HANDS-ON: 15 minutes
TOTAL: 27 minutes, plus 8 hours to chill
MAKES: 36 cookies

- ¾ cup (3 ⅓ ounces) all-purpose flour
- ¾ cup (3 ½ ounces) whole-wheat flour
- ¾ cup old-fashioned rolled oats
- ½ teaspoon baking powder
- ¼ teaspoon baking soda
- ¼ teaspoon salt
- ¼ cup dried cranberries
- 2½ tablespoons finely chopped walnuts
- 2½ tablespoons semisweet chocolate minichips
- ¾ cup packed brown sugar
- 2½ ounces (⅓ cup) butter, softened
- 2 tablespoons honey
- ¾ teaspoon vanilla extract
- 1 large egg
- 1 large egg white
- Cooking spray

1. Stir together the flours, oats, baking powder, and next 5 ingredients in a large bowl.

2. Put the sugar and butter in a large bowl. Beat with an electric mixer at medium speed until light and fluffy. Add the honey, vanilla, egg, and egg white; beat well. Add the flour mixture to the sugar mixture; beat at low speed until well blended. Cover and chill 8 hours or overnight.

3. Preheat the oven to 350°F. Coat baking sheets with the cooking spray.

4. Drop the batter by tablespoonfuls onto the prepared baking sheet. Bake at 350°F for 10 minutes. Cool 2 minutes on pans. Transfer to wire racks. Cool completely.

MAKE
Substitute any nut for the chopped walnuts.

ULTIMATE CHOCOLATE CHIP COOKIES

HANDS-ON: 45 minutes
TOTAL: 45 minutes
MAKES: 5 dozen cookies

Cooking spray
- 6 ounces (¾ cup) butter, softened
- ¾ cup granulated sugar
- ¾ cup firmly packed dark brown sugar
- 2 large eggs
- 1½ teaspoons vanilla extract
- 2¼ cups (10.1 ounces) plus 2 tablespoons all-purpose flour
- 1 teaspoon baking soda
- ¾ teaspoon salt
- 1 (12-ounce) package semisweet chocolate chips

1. Preheat the oven to 350°F. Lightly grease baking sheets with the cooking spray. Put the butter and sugars in a large bowl. Beat with an electric mixer at medium speed until creamy. Add the eggs and vanilla, beating until blended.

2. Stir together the flour, baking soda, and salt in a small bowl; gradually add to butter mixture, beating well. Stir in the chips. Drop by tablespoonfuls onto the prepared baking sheets.

3. Bake at 350°F for 8 to 14 minutes or until desired degree of doneness. Transfer to wire racks; cool completely.

Pecan-Chocolate Chip Cookies: Add 1½ cups chopped, toasted pecans with chips. Proceed as directed.

Oatmeal-Raisin Chocolate Chip Cookies: Reduce flour to 2 cups. Add 1 cup uncooked quick-cooking oats to dry ingredients and 1 cup raisins with chips. Proceed as directed.

Almond-Toffee Chocolate Chip Cookies: Reduce morsels to 1 cup. Add ½ cup slivered toasted almonds and 1 cup almond toffee bits. Proceed as directed.

Dark Chocolate Chip Cookies: Substitute 1 (12-ounce) package dark chocolate chips for semisweet chocolate chips. Proceed as directed.

COCONUT MACAROONS WITH BITTERSWEET CHOCOLATE AND PISTACHIOS

HANDS-ON: 16 minutes
TOTAL: 1 hour, 33 minutes
MAKES: 21 cookies

Parchment paper
- ¼ **teaspoon cream of tartar**
- 2 **large egg whites**
- 3 **tablespoons granulated sugar**
- ¼ **teaspoon vanilla extract**

Pinch of salt
- 2 **cups flaked sweetened coconut**
- ½ **cup bittersweet chocolate chips**
- ¼ **cup finely chopped pistachios**

1. Preheat the oven to 325°F. Line a baking sheet with the parchment paper.

2. Put the cream of tartar and egg whites in a large bowl. Beat with an electric mixer at high speed until foamy. Gradually add the sugar, vanilla, and salt, beating at high speed until foamy and opaque, about 1 minute. Fold the coconut into the egg white mixture using a rubber spatula.

3. Spoon the egg white mixture by tablespoonfuls 2 inches apart onto the prepared baking sheet. Bake at 325°F for 20 minutes or until edges are golden brown. Cool completely on the baking sheet on a wire rack.

4. Put the chocolate chips in a small microwave-safe bowl; microwave at HIGH 45 seconds or until the chips melt, stirring until smooth. Dip top of each macaroon into the chocolate, and sprinkle with the pistachios. Let the cookies set (about 20 to 30 minutes).

MOROCCAN SPICED SANDWICH COOKIES

HANDS-ON: 1 hour, 10 minutes
TOTAL: 3 hours
MAKES: 16 sandwich cookies

- 8 ounces (1 cup) butter, softened
- 1 cup powdered sugar
- 1 large egg
- 2 teaspoons grated orange zest
- 2 cups (9 ounces) all-purpose flour
- ½ teaspoon ground anise
- ¼ teaspoon salt
- ½ cup finely chopped unsalted pistachios
- ¾ cup vanilla creamy ready-to-spread frosting (from 1-pound container)

1. Put the butter in a large bowl. Beat with an electric mixer at medium speed until creamy. Gradually add the powdered sugar; beat until light and fluffy. Add the egg and 1½ teaspoons of the orange zest; beat well. Gradually add the flour, anise, and salt; beat until combined. Stir in the nuts. Cover with plastic wrap; chill 1 hour.

2. Preheat oven to 350°F. Place the dough on a lightly floured surface, and roll to ¼-inch thickness. Cut with a 2-inch 8-point star-shaped cookie cutter, rerolling dough once. Place 1 inch apart on ungreased baking sheets.

3. Bake at 350°F for 12 to 14 minutes or until firm to the touch. Immediately transfer the cookies to wire racks. Cool completely (about 20 minutes).

4. Stir together the frosting and remaining ½ teaspoon orange zest. For each sandwich cookie, spread about 1 teaspoon of the frosting onto the bottom side of 1 cookie. Top with the second cookie, bottom side down; gently press together. Let stand until set. Store tightly covered at room temperature.

GINGER SHORTBREAD COOKIES WITH LEMON-CREAM CHEESE FROSTING

HANDS-ON: 25 minutes
TOTAL: 2 hours, 20 minutes
MAKES: about 2 dozen cookies

Cookies:
Parchment paper

- 8 ounces (1 cup) butter, softened
- ½ cup granulated sugar
- ¼ teaspoon vanilla extract
- 2¼ cups (10.1 ounces) all-purpose flour
- 2 tablespoons minced crystallized ginger
- ⅛ teaspoon salt

Lemon-Cream Cheese Frosting:
- ½ (8-ounce) package cream cheese, softened
- 2 ounces (¼ cup) butter, softened
- 2 cups powdered sugar
- 1 teaspoon grated lemon zest
- 1 teaspoon fresh lemon juice

1. Make the cookies: Preheat the oven to 275°F. Line 2 baking sheets with the parchment paper. Put the butter in the bowl of a heavy-duty electric stand mixer. Beat at medium speed until creamy; gradually add the sugar, beating well. Stir in the vanilla.

2. Stir together the flour, ginger, and salt; gradually add to the butter mixture, beating at low speed until blended after each addition.

3. Place the dough on a lightly floured surface, and roll the dough to a ¼-inch thickness. Cut with a 2-inch round cutter. Place 2 inches apart on the prepared baking sheets (about 12 per sheet). Reroll scraps once.

4. Bake, in batches, at 275°F for 40 minutes or until lightly browned on bottom. (Refrigerate the second batch while baking the first batch.) Cool on baking sheet 2 minutes. Transfer to a wire rack, and cool completely (about 30 minutes).

5. Make the frosting: Place the cream cheese and butter in a large bowl. Beat with an electric mixer at medium-high speed until light and fluffy. Gradually add sugar, and beat well. Stir in the zest and juice. Spread about 1 tablespoon on each cooled cookie, using a small spatula.

SWEET AND SALTY PEANUT-CHOCOLATE CHUNK COOKIES

HANDS-ON: 10 minutes
TOTAL: 30 minutes
MAKES: 38 cookies

- ⅓ cup coarsely chopped unsalted, dry-roasted peanuts
- 1 cup (4.5 ounces) all-purpose flour
- ½ teaspoon baking powder
- ¼ teaspoon baking soda
- ½ cup granulated sugar
- ½ cup packed brown sugar
- 2 ounces (¼ cup) unsalted butter, softened
- 1 teaspoon vanilla extract
- 1 large egg
- ⅓ cup semisweet chocolate chips
- ½ teaspoon coarse sea salt

Cooking spray

1. Preheat the oven to 350°F.

2. Put the nuts in a small baking pan. Bake at 350°F for 8 minutes or until lightly toasted; cool.

3. Stir together the flour, baking powder, and baking soda well with a whisk.

4. Place the sugars and butter in a large bowl. Beat with an electric mixer at medium speed until well blended (about 2 minutes). Add the vanilla and egg; beat until combined. Add the flour mixture to the sugar mixture; beat at low speed until well blended. Stir in the peanuts, chocolate chips, and salt.

5. Coat baking sheets with the cooking spray. Drop the dough by teaspoonfuls 2 inches apart onto the prepared baking sheets. Bake at 350°F for 10 minutes or until edges are lightly browned. Cool on the baking sheets 5 minutes. Transfer cookies to wire racks. Cool completely.

 **MAKE** | Use lightly greased spoons to make the drop cookies.

WHITE CHOCOLATE PRETZEL COOKIES

HANDS-ON: 45 minutes
TOTAL: 45 minutes
MAKES: 5 dozen cookies

Parchment paper

- 2¼ cups (10.1 ounces) all-purpose flour plus 2 tablespoons
- 1 teaspoon baking soda
- ¾ teaspoon salt
- 6 ounces (¾ cup) butter, softened
- ¾ cup granulated sugar
- ¾ cup packed dark brown sugar
- 2 large eggs
- 1½ teaspoons vanilla extract
- 18 ounces (1½ packages) semisweet chocolate chips
- 1 (7-ounce) package white chocolate-covered mini-pretzel twists, coarsely crushed

1. Preheat the oven to 350°F. Line the baking sheets with the parchment paper. Stir together the flour, baking soda, and salt.

2. Put the butter, sugars in a large bowl. Beat with an electric mixer at medium speed until light and fluffy. Beat in the eggs and vanilla. Gradually add the flour mixture to the butter mixture, beating at low speed just until blended. Stir in the chocolate chips and pretzels.

3. Drop the dough by tablespoonfuls 1 to 2 inches apart onto the prepared baking sheets.

4. Bake at 350°F for 10 to 14 minutes. Immediately transfer to wire racks, and cool completely (about 20 minutes).

CHUNKY CHOCOLATE GOBS

HANDS-ON: 35 minutes
TOTAL: 1 hour, 30 minutes
MAKES: about 2½ dozen cookies

- 6 ounces (¾ cup) unsalted butter, softened
- ⅓ cup butter-flavored shortening
- 1 cup granulated sugar
- ⅔ cup firmly packed dark brown sugar
- 2 large eggs
- 2 teaspoons vanilla extract
- 2 cups (9 ounces) all-purpose flour
- ⅔ cup unsweetened cocoa
- 1 teaspoon baking soda
- ¼ teaspoon salt
- 2 cups cream-filled chocolate sandwich cookies, coarsely chopped (16 cookies)
- 3 (1.75-ounce) dark-chocolate covered coconut candy bars, chilled and chopped
- 1 to 2 cups semisweet chocolate chips

Parchment paper

1. Put the butter and shortening in a large bowl. Beat with an electric mixer at medium speed until creamy; gradually add sugars, beating until light and fluffy. Add the eggs and vanilla, beating until blended.

2. Stir together the flour and next 3 ingredients; gradually add to the butter mixture, beating until blended. Stir in the cookies, candy bars, and desired amount of chocolate chips. Chill the dough 30 minutes.

3. Preheat the oven to 350°F. Line baking sheets with the parchment paper. Drop the dough by ¼ cupfuls 2 inches apart onto the prepared baking sheets. Bake at 350°F for 10 to 12 minutes or until barely set. Cool on the baking sheets 10 minutes. Transfer to wire racks, and cool completely (about 20 minutes).

DOUBLE-CHOCOLATE COOKIES

HANDS-ON: 16 minutes
TOTAL: 1 hour, 15 minutes
MAKES: 26 cookies

1½ cups (6.75 ounces) unbleached all-purpose flour

6 tablespoons unsweetened cocoa

⅜ teaspoon salt

¾ cup sugar

2 ounces (¼ cup) unsalted butter, softened

2 tablespoons canola oil

2 large eggs

¼ teaspoon vanilla extract

½ cup bittersweet chocolate chips

Parchment paper

TIP: Unsweetened chocolate is a baking staple. It deepens chocolate flavor without adding more sweetness.

1. Stir together the flour, cocoa, and salt in a bowl with a whisk.

2. Put the sugar, butter, and oil in a bowl. Beat with an electric mixer at medium speed until well combined (about 5 minutes). Add the eggs, 1 at a time, beating well after each addition. Add the vanilla; beat 1 minute. Add the flour mixture to the butter mixture, beating at low speed just until combined. Add the chocolate chips; beat at low speed just until combined. Cover with plastic wrap; chill 30 minutes.

3. Preheat the oven to 350°F. Line baking sheets with the parchment paper.

4. Drop the dough by 1½ tablespoonfuls 2 inches apart onto the prepared baking sheets. Bake at 350°F for 8 minutes or until almost set. Cool on the baking sheets 2 minutes or until firm. Transfer the cookies to wire racks. Cool.

SPICED ALMOND-CHOCOLATE CRINKLES

HANDS-ON: 1 hour, 30 minutes
TOTAL: 2 hours, 30 minutes
MAKES: 5 dozen cookies

- 2 ounces (¼ cup) butter
- 4 ounces unsweetened chocolate, chopped
- 4 large eggs
- 2 cups (9 ounces) all-purpose flour
- 2 cups granulated sugar
- ½ cup chopped almonds
- 2 teaspoons baking powder
- ½ teaspoon salt
- ½ teaspoon ground ginger
- ½ teaspoon ground cinnamon
- ¼ teaspoon ground cloves

Cooking spray
- ¾ cup powdered sugar

1. Melt the butter and chocolate in a 3-quart saucepan over low heat until smooth, stirring constantly. Remove from the heat, and cool for 5 minutes.

2. Add the eggs to the chocolate mixture, beating with a spoon until well blended. Add the next 8 ingredients except the cooking spray and powdered sugar, stirring until well blended. Cover the dough with plastic wrap; chill at least 1 hour for easier handling.

3. Preheat the oven to 300°F. Coat baking sheets with the cooking spray. Put the powdered sugar in a small bowl. Shape the dough into 60 (1-inch) balls; roll in the powdered sugar, coating heavily. Place the balls 2 inches apart on the prepared baking sheets.

4. Bake at 300°F for 13 to 18 minutes or until set. Immediately transfer to wire racks, and cool completely (about 20 minutes).

BROWNIE COOKIES

HANDS-ON: 1 hour
TOTAL: 1 hour
MAKES: 30 cookies

Parchment paper

- 2 cups chopped pecans
- 4 ounces (½ cup) butter, cut into pieces
- 4 ounces unsweetened chocolate, chopped
- 3 cups semisweet chocolate chips (18 ounces)
- 1½ cups (6.75 ounces) all-purpose flour
- ½ teaspoon baking powder
- ½ teaspoon salt
- 4 large eggs
- 1½ cups granulated sugar
- 2 teaspoons vanilla extract

TIP: For a fudgy texture, it's ok to slightly underbake these cookies.

1. Preheat the oven to 350°F. Line the baking sheets with the parchment paper. Spread the pecans in an ungreased shallow pan. Bake, uncovered, at 350°F for 6 to 10 minutes, stirring occasionally, until light brown.

2. Put the butter, chopped chocolate, and 1½ cups of the chocolate chips in a 3-quart heavy saucepan; cook over low heat, stirring constantly, until the butter and chocolate are melted. Remove from the heat; cool.

3. Stir together the flour, baking powder, and salt in a medium bowl. Put the eggs, sugar, and vanilla in a large bowl. Beat with an electric mixer at medium speed until well blended. Gradually beat in the flour mixture at low speed. Add the chocolate mixture; beat well. Stir in the toasted pecans and the remaining chocolate chips. Drop the dough by 2 tablespoonfuls 1 inch apart onto the prepared baking sheets.

4. Bake at 350°F for 10 minutes. Cool on the baking sheets 2 minutes. Transfer to wire racks.

PECAN CRESCENTS

HANDS-ON: 30 minutes
TOTAL: 45 minutes
MAKES: about 5 dozen cookies

1 cup pecan halves, toasted

8 ounces (1 cup) butter, softened

2¾ cups powdered sugar

2 teaspoons vanilla extract

2½ cups (11.25 ounces) sifted all-purpose flour

1. Pulse the pecans in a food processor until they are coarse like sand.

2. Put the butter and ¾ cup of the powdered sugar in a large bowl. Beat with an electric mixer at medium speed until creamy. Beat in the vanilla and ground pecans. Gradually add the flour, beating until a soft dough forms. Cover and chill 1 hour.

3. Preheat the oven to 350°F. Divide the dough into 5 portions; divide each portion into 12 pieces. Roll the dough pieces into 2-inch logs, curving the ends to form crescents. Place on ungreased baking sheets.

4. Bake at 350°F for 10 to 12 minutes or until lightly browned. Cool on the baking sheets 5 minutes. Put the remaining 2 cups powdered sugar in a bowl. Roll the warm cookies in the powdered sugar. Cool completely on wire racks, and roll cookies in remaining powdered sugar again after cooled.

PECAN COOKIES

Hands-on: 45 minutes
Total: 3 hours, 12 minutes
Makes: 40 cookies

- 2 cups (9 ounces) all-purpose flour
- ½ teaspoon salt
- ¼ teaspoon baking powder
- 5 ounces (⅔ cup) butter
- ⅔ cup granulated sugar
- 1 large egg
- 1½ teaspoons vanilla extract
- ¾ cup chopped toasted pecans

Parchment paper

- ⅓ cup powdered sugar

1. Stir together the flour, salt, and baking powder with a whisk. Put the butter and granulated sugar in a large bowl. Beat with an electric mixer at high speed until light and fluffy. Add the egg, and beat until well blended. Beat in the vanilla. Reduce mixer speed to low. Add the flour mixture and beat just until combined. Stir in the pecans.

2. Shape the dough into a 4-inch round, and cover with plastic wrap. Chill 1 hour.

3. Preheat oven to 350°F. Line a baking sheet with the parchment paper. Roll the dough to ¼-inch thickness on a lightly floured surface. Cut out 40 (2- x 3-inch) cookies, rerolling the scraps as necessary. Place the cookies 1 inch apart on the prepared baking sheet. Bake at 350°F for 9 minutes or until lightly browned on bottoms. Cool on a wire rack.

4. Dust the cooled cookies with powdered sugar.

TIP: Dust the cookies with a bit of powdered sugar for a finishing touch that's not too sweet. Place the sugar in a fine sieve, and shake it over the cooled cookies.

RASPBERRY LINZER COOKIES

HANDS-ON: 25 minutes
TOTAL: 1 hour, 35 minutes
MAKES: 3 dozen cookies

- 1½ cups plus 2 tablespoons (7.5 ounces) all-purpose flour
- 1 cup whole blanched almonds
- ½ teaspoon baking powder
- ½ teaspoon ground cinnamon
- ¼ teaspoon salt
- ⅔ cup granulated sugar
- 4 ounces (½ cup) unsalted butter, softened
- ½ teaspoon grated lemon zest
- 4 large egg yolks
- Plastic wrap
- Parchment paper
- 6 tablespoons raspberry preserves with seeds
- 2 teaspoons powdered sugar

1. Put ½ cup of the flour and the almonds in a food processor; process until finely ground. Whisk the almond mixture, remaining flour, baking powder, cinnamon, and salt in a bowl. Put the granulated sugar, butter, and zest in a large bowl. Beat with an electric mixer at medium speed until light and fluffy. Add the egg yolks; beat until well blended. Beating at low speed, gradually add flour mixture; beat just until a soft dough forms. Turn the dough out onto a sheet of plastic wrap; knead lightly 3 times or until smooth. Divide the dough into 2 equal portions; wrap each portion in plastic wrap. Chill 1 hour.

2. Preheat the oven to 350°F. Line baking sheets with the parchment paper. Place each dough portion on a floured surface. Roll into a ⅛-inch thickness; cut with a 2-inch rectangular cookie cutter with fluted edges to form 36 cookies. Repeat procedure with the remaining dough portion; use a 1-inch rectangular fluted cutter to remove centers of 36 rectangles. Arrange 1 inch apart on the prepared baking sheets. Bake, 1 batch at a time, at 350°F for 10 minutes or until edges are lightly browned. Cool on the baking sheets 5 minutes. Transfer to wire racks. Cool completely.

3. Spread the center of each whole cookie with about ½ teaspoon preserves. Sprinkle the cutout cookies with powdered sugar. Place 1 cutout cookie on top of each whole cookie.

PEPPERMINT CRESCENTS

HANDS-ON: 50 minutes
TOTAL: 1 hour, 35 minutes
MAKES: 3 dozen cookies

- 8 ounces (1 cup) butter, softened
- 2⅔ cups powdered sugar
- 1¼ teaspoons peppermint extract
- ⅛ teaspoon salt
- 2½ cups (11.25 ounces) all-purpose flour
- Cooking spray
- 2½ tablespoons milk
- Coarsely crushed hard peppermint candies

1. Put the butter in a large bowl. Beat with an electric mixer at medium speed until creamy. Add ⅔ cup of the powdered sugar, 1 teaspoon of the peppermint extract, and salt; beat well. Gradually add the flour, beating at low speed just until blended. Divide the dough into thirds. Cover; chill 30 minutes.

2. Preheat the oven to 325°F. Lightly coat baking sheets with the cooking spray.

3. Working with 1 portion of the dough at a time, divide each portion into 12 pieces. Roll each piece into a 2-inch log; curve the ends of each to form a crescent shape. Place the crescents 2 inches apart on the prepared baking sheets.

4. Bake at 325°F for 18 minutes or until light golden brown. Cool on the baking sheets 1 minute. Put 1 cup of the powdered sugar in a small bowl; carefully roll the warm cookies in the powdered sugar. Place on wire racks, and cool completely (about 20 minutes).

5. Stir together the remaining 1 cup powdered sugar, the milk, and the remaining ¼ teaspoon peppermint extract. Drizzle over the cookies; sprinkle with the crushed candies, pressing gently. Let stand until set. Store tightly covered at room temperature.

TINSEL COOKIES

HANDS-ON: 50 minutes
TOTAL: 1 hour, 25 minutes
MAKES: 40 cookies

8 ounces (1 cup) butter, softened

1 cup powdered sugar

1 teaspoon rum extract

1 teaspoon vanilla extract

2 cups (9 ounces) all-purpose flour

¼ teaspoon salt

Parchment paper

½ cup silver decorator sugar crystals

1. Put the butter in a large bowl. Beat with an electric mixer at medium speed until creamy. Add the powdered sugar, rum extract, and vanilla; beat at low speed until creamy. Gradually add the flour and salt, beating at low speed until combined. Cover and chill 30 minutes.

2. Preheat the oven to 350°F. Line baking sheets with the parchment paper. Put the sugar crystals in a small bowl. Shape the dough into 40 (1-inch) balls. Gently roll the balls in sugar crystals. Place the balls 1 inch apart on the prepared baking sheets.

3. Bake at 350°F for 12 to 15 minutes or until light golden on the bottom but pale on the top. Cool on the baking sheets 2 minutes. Transfer to wire racks, and cool completely (about 20 minutes).

CARAMEL-APPLE-OATMEAL COOKIES

HANDS-ON: 15 minutes
TOTAL: 27 minutes
MAKES: 4 dozen cookies

Parchment paper

- 1½ cups (6.75 ounces) all-purpose flour
- 1½ cups old-fashioned rolled oats
- 1 teaspoon baking powder
- ½ teaspoon baking soda
- ½ teaspoon salt
- ¾ cup granulated sugar
- ¾ cup packed brown sugar
- 6 ounces (⅓ cup) unsalted butter, softened
- 2 teaspoons vanilla extract
- 1 large egg
- ¾ cup finely chopped dried apple slices
- ¾ cup caramel bits or 16 small soft caramel candies, chopped

1. Preheat the oven to 350°F. Line baking sheets with the parchment paper.

2. Put the flour and next 4 ingredients in a bowl; stir well.

3. Put the sugars and butter in a large bowl. Beat with an electric mixer at medium speed until light and fluffy. Add the vanilla and egg; beat well. Gradually add the flour mixture; beat at low speed until just combined. Fold in the apple and caramel bits.

4. Drop the dough by 2 teaspoonfuls 2 inches apart onto the prepared baking sheets. Flatten the dough slightly with your hand. Bake at 350°F for 9 minutes. Cool on the baking sheets 3 minutes. Transfer to wire racks. Cool completely.

MAKE

Mix it up by adding mini chocolate chips with the caramel bits.

HONEY-ORANGE-GINGER COOKIES

HANDS-ON: 40 minutes
TOTAL: 1 hour, 10 minutes
MAKES: 48 cookies

2¼ cups (10.1 ounces) all-purpose flour

1 tablespoon grated orange zest

1 teaspoon ground ginger

½ teaspoon baking soda

½ teaspoon baking powder

4 ounces (½ cup) butter, softened

⅔ cup granulated sugar

½ cup honey

1 teaspoon orange extract

1 large egg

Additional sugar

1. Stir together the flour, orange zest, ginger, baking soda, and baking powder in a medium bowl. Put the butter and ⅔ cup sugar in a large bowl. Beat with an electric mixer at medium speed until creamy. Add the honey, orange extract, and egg; beat until blended. Gradually beat in the flour mixture at low speed just until blended. Cover; chill 30 minutes to 1 hour.

2. Preheat the oven to 350°F. Put the additional sugar in a small bowl. Shape the dough into 1-inch balls; roll in the additional sugar. Place the balls 2 inches apart on the ungreased baking sheets; flatten slightly with the bottom of a glass.

3. Bake at 350°F for 8 to 10 minutes or until lightly browned. Transfer to wire racks.

COCONUT-MACADAMIA SHORTBREAD

Hands-on: 45 minutes
Total: 4 hours, 45 minutes
Makes: 48 cookies

2 cups (9 ounces) all-purpose flour

¼ teaspoon baking powder

⅛ teaspoon salt

8 ounces (1 cup) butter, softened

¾ cup powdered sugar

2 teaspoons vanilla extract

¼ teaspoon coconut extract

1 cup flaked sweetened coconut, toasted

½ cup finely chopped macadamia nuts

Waxed paper

Cooking spray or parchment paper

1. Stir together the flour, baking powder, and salt in a medium bowl. Put the butter in a large bowl. Beat with an electric mixer at medium speed until creamy. Gradually add the powdered sugar, beating until smooth. Stir in the vanilla and coconut extract until blended. Beat in the flour mixture at low speed until blended. Stir in the coconut and nuts.

2. Shape the dough into 2 (7-inch) logs. Wrap in the waxed paper; chill 4 hours.

3. Preheat the oven to 350°F. Coat baking sheets with cooking spray or line with parchment paper. Unwrap the dough; cut each log into 24 slices. Place the slices 1 inch apart on the prepared baking sheets.

4. Bake at 350°F for 10 to 12 minutes or until the edges are golden. Transfer to wire racks. Store the cooled cookies tightly covered.

MAKE | Dough logs can be frozen in zip-top plastic freezer bags up to 1 month. Remove from freezer 10 minutes before cutting and baking.

SUGAR COOKIE MACAROON SANDWICHES

HANDS-ON: 1 hour, 20 minutes
TOTAL: 2 hours
MAKES: 2 dozen cookies

Parchment paper

- 1 (17.5-ounce) pouch sugar cookie mix
- 4 ounces (½ cup) butter, softened
- 3 cups flaked sweetened coconut
- 1 large egg
- 4 ounces semisweet chocolate, chopped
- 2 tablespoons whipping cream

1. Preheat the oven to 350°F. Line the baking sheets with the parchment paper.

2. Put the sugar cookie mix, butter, coconut, and egg in a large bowl. Beat with an electric mixer at medium speed until a soft dough forms. Shape the dough into 48 (1-inch) balls. Place the balls 2 inches apart on the prepared baking sheets; flatten slightly.

3. Bake at 350°F for 10 to 12 minutes or until the bottoms are golden. Cool 5 minutes. Transfer to wire racks, and cool completely (about 20 minutes).

4. Put the chocolate and whipping cream in a small microwave-safe bowl; microwave, uncovered, at HIGH 30 seconds; stir. Microwave 30 seconds longer, stirring after 15 seconds, or until the chocolate can be stirred smooth. For each sandwich cookie, spread about 1 teaspoon of the chocolate mixture on the bottom of 1 cookie. Top with a second cookie, bottom side down; gently press together. Let stand until the chocolate is set.

LEMON MELTAWAYS

HANDS-ON: 30 minutes
TOTAL: 2 hours
MAKES: about 3 1/2 dozen cookies

- 6 ounces (¾ cup) plus 2 tablespoons butter, softened
- 1½ cups powdered sugar
- 1 tablespoon grated lemon zest
- 2 tablespoons fresh lemon juice
- 1½ cups (6.75 ounces) all-purpose flour
- ¼ cup cornstarch
- ¼ teaspoon salt

Parchment paper

1. Put the butter in the bowl of a heavy-duty electric stand mixer. Beat at medium speed until creamy. Add ½ cup of the powdered sugar; beat at medium speed until light and fluffy. Stir in the zest and juice. Stir together the flour, cornstarch, and salt with a whisk. Gradually add the flour mixture to the butter mixture, beating at low speed just until blended. Cover and chill 1 hour.

2. Preheat the oven to 350°F. Line baking sheets with the parchment paper. Drop the dough by level spoonfuls 2 inches apart onto the prepared baking sheets, using a 1-inch cookie scoop.

3. Bake at 350°F for 13 minutes or until lightly browned around the edges. Cool on the baking sheets 5 minutes.

4. Toss together the warm cookies and remaining 1 cup powdered sugar in a small bowl.

SNOWMAN COOKIES, PAGE 70

CHAPTER 3

DECORATED COOKIES

- -

PERFECT FOR THE KIDS, THIS COLLECTION
OF COOKIES IS A BLAST TO MAKE TOGETHER.

SNOWMAN COOKIES

- -

HANDS-ON: 25 minutes
TOTAL: 1 hour, 25 minutes
MAKES: 2 dozen cookies

- 1 (16.5-ounce) package refrigerated sugar cookie dough
- ¼ cup (1.1 ounces) all-purpose flour
- 1 (7-ounce) pouch white cookie decorating icing

White and black sparkling sugar

- 1 (7-ounce) pouch green cookie decorating icing
- 1 (7-ounce) pouch blue cookie decorating icing
- 1 (4.25-ounce) tube black cookie decorating icing
- 1 (4.25-ounce) tube red cookie decorating icing
- 24 snowflake candy sprinkles
- 1 ounce orange fondant
- 72 red cinnamon candies

Waxed paper or aluminum foil

1. Preheat the oven to 375°F. Break up the cookie dough into a medium bowl. Knead in the flour with your hands until well blended.

2. Place the dough on a lightly floured surface, and roll to ¼-inch thickness. Cut with a floured 4-inch snowman-shaped cookie cutter. Place 1 inch apart on ungreased baking sheets.

3. Bake at 375°F for 7 to 9 minutes or until the edges are light golden brown. Cool on the baking sheets 2 minutes. Transfer to wire racks, and cool completely (about 20 minutes).

4. Spread the white icing onto the cookies. Sprinkle the white sugar onto the bodies and faces of the snowmen; sprinkle the black sugar onto the hats. Use the green and blue icing to add scarves. Use the black decorating icing to add eyes and mouths. Use the red decorating icing to add hatbands; place 1 snowflake sprinkle on each hatband. Shape the orange fondant into 24 very small nose shapes; add 1 nose to each snowman. Add 3 cinnamon candies to each snowman for buttons. Let stand until the icing is set. Store between layers of waxed paper or aluminum foil.

STOCKING SUGAR COOKIES

HANDS-ON: 30 minutes
TOTAL: 1 hour
MAKES: 2½ dozen cookies

2½ cups (10.1 ounces) all-purpose flour

1 teaspoon baking powder

¼ teaspoon salt

6 ounces (¾ cup) butter, softened

1 cup granulated sugar

2 large eggs

½ teaspoon vanilla extract

¼ teaspoon almond extract

1 (7-ounce) pouch red cookie decorating icing

1 (7-ounce) pouch green cookie decorating icing

1 (7-ounce) pouch white cookie decorating icing

Red, green, and white sanding sugar

1. Stir together the flour, baking powder, and salt.

2. Put the butter and granulated sugar in a large bowl. Beat with an electric mixer at medium speed until smooth. Beat in the eggs, 1 at a time, until blended. Beat in the vanilla and almond extracts. Gradually add the flour mixture to butter mixture, beating at low speed just until blended. Shape the dough into a ball; wrap in plastic wrap. Chill 2 hours or until firm.

3. Preheat the oven to 375°F. Place the dough on a lightly floured surface, and roll to ¼-inch thickness. Cut with a floured 3-inch stocking-shaped cookie cutter. Place 1 inch apart on ungreased baking sheets.

4. Bake at 375°F for 10 to 12 minutes or until set. Cool on the baking sheets 2 minutes. Transfer to wire racks, and cool completely (about 20 minutes).

5. Decorate using the icing and sanding sugar.

ROLL-OUT HOLIDAY COOKIES

HANDS-ON: 24 minutes
TOTAL: 2 hours, 39 minutes
MAKES: 30 cookies

Cookies:
- ¾ cup (3.9 ounces) white rice flour
- 2.6 ounces potato starch (about ½ cup)
- ¼ cup (1.05 ounces) tapioca flour
- ½ teaspoon baking powder
- ½ teaspoon xanthan gum
- ½ cup granulated sugar
- 3 ounces (⅓ cup) butter, softened
- 1½ teaspoons vanilla extract
- 1 teaspoon 1% low-fat milk
- 1 large egg

Parchment paper

Frosting:
- 1 cup powdered sugar
- 1½ tablespoons 1% low-fat milk
- ¼ teaspoon vanilla extract
- 1 tablespoon sugar sprinkles

TIP: This is a great cookie for those with gluten sensitivities.

1. **Make the cookies:** Sift together the white rice flour, potato starch, tapioca flour, baking powder, and xanthan gum.

2. Put the granulated sugar and butter in a medium bowl. Beat with an electric mixer at medium speed until light and fluffy. Add 1½ teaspoons vanilla, 1 teaspoon milk, and egg, beating until blended. Add the flour mixture, stirring until blended. Shape the dough into a ball; wrap in plastic wrap. Chill 1 hour.

3. Preheat the oven to 375°F. Line baking sheets with the parchment paper.

4. Unwrap the dough; place on a lightly floured surface. Roll the dough to a ⅛-inch thickness. Cut into 30 cookies with a 2-inch round cookie cutter, rerolling scraps as necessary. Place cookies 1 inch apart on the prepared baking sheets. Bake at 375° for 10 minutes or until lightly browned around the edges. Transfer to a wire rack; cool completely.

5. **Make the frosting:** Stir together the powdered sugar, 1½ tablespoons milk, and ¼ teaspoon vanilla in a small bowl with a whisk until smooth. Spread 1 teaspoon frosting on each cookie; top with the sprinkles. Place the cookies on the wire rack until set.

REINDEER TREATS

HANDS-ON: 20 minutes
TOTAL: 35 minutes
MAKES: 2 dozen treats

Waxed paper

- 12 ounces vanilla candy coating, chopped
- 24 miniature caramel corn-flavored rice cakes
- 48 mini-pretzel twists
- 48 chocolate chips
- 24 red cinnamon candies

1. Line a baking sheet with the waxed paper. Melt the candy coating in a saucepan over low heat, stirring constantly.

2. Dip a rice cake in the candy coating; place on the prepared baking sheet. Dip rounded side of 2 pretzels in candy coating; place on the baking sheet on each side of the rice cake to look like antlers.

3. Add the chocolate chips for eyes and a cinnamon candy for nose. Repeat the procedure with the remaining rice cakes, candy coating, pretzels, chocolate chips, and cinnamon candies. Let stand 15 minutes or until set. Carefully remove from the waxed paper; store tightly covered at room temperature.

CHRISTMAS COOKIE TREES

HANDS-ON: 1 hour
TOTAL: 1 hour
MAKES: 5 cookie trees

Parchment paper

  1 (16.5-ounce) roll refrigerated
    sugar cookie dough

  ¼ cup (1.1 ounces) all-purpose flour

  2 (12-ounce) containers white
    whipped ready-to-spread frosting

Yellow food coloring paste

Green food coloring paste

Yellow sanding sugar, red and white
  candy sprinkles, coarse sugar

TIP: Make the sugar cookies ahead of time for easy assembly with the kids.

1. Preheat the oven to 350°. Line 2 baking sheets with the parchment paper. Break up the cookie dough; knead in the flour with your hands until blended.

2. Place the dough on a floured surface, and roll to ⅛-inch thickness. Cut out 5 stars with a 1¼-inch star-shaped cutter. Using flower-shaped cutters in 5 different sizes (3½, 3¼, 2¾, 2¼, and 1½-inch), cut 25 cookies, 5 of each size.

3. Place the stars and the smaller flowers 1 inch apart on 1 baking sheet. Place the larger flowers 2 inches apart on the second baking sheet. Bake smaller cookies at 350° for 6 to 8 minutes and the larger cookies 8 to 10 minutes, or until lightly browned. Transfer to wire racks, and cool completely (about 10 minutes).

4. Stir together 2 tablespoons of the frosting and the yellow food coloring. Frost the star cookies with the yellow frosting; sprinkle with the yellow sugar.

5. Stir together the remaining frosting and green food coloring. Spoon into a zip-top plastic freezer bag. Snip 1 corner of the bag to make a small hole. Pipe the green frosting on each large flower cookie; stack each with 4 cookies, largest to smallest, piping frosting on each cookie before layering. Top each tree with a star cookie, and decorate with candy sprinkles and coarse sugar.

GINGERBREAD COOKIES

HANDS-ON: 30 minutes
TOTAL: 1 hour
MAKES: 5 dozen cookies

Parchment paper
  2 cups (9.2 ounces) brown rice flour
  ½ cup (2.6 ounces) white rice flour
  ¼ cup (1.05 ounces) tapioca flour
  1.15 ounces cornstarch (about ¼ cup)
  1½ teaspoons baking soda
  1 teaspoon xanthan gum
  1 teaspoon ground ginger
  1 teaspoon ground cinnamon
  ¼ teaspoon salt
  ¼ teaspoon ground nutmeg
  ¼ teaspoon ground cloves
  ¼ teaspoon ground allspice
  4 ounces (½ cup) butter, softened
  ½ cup packed light brown sugar
  ¼ cup granulated sugar
  ½ cup light molasses
  1 large egg
Cooking spray
  1 teaspoon granulated sugar

1. Preheat the oven to 375°F. Line baking sheets with the parchment paper.

2. Stir together the flours, cornstarch, baking soda, and next 7 ingredients in a medium bowl with a whisk.

3. Put the butter, brown sugar, and ¼ cup granulated sugar in a large bowl. Beat with an electric mixer at low speed 1 to 2 minutes; increase speed to medium, and beat until well blended. Add the molasses and egg; beat well. Gradually add the flour mixture, beating until well blended.

4. Lightly coat your hands with the cooking spray; shape the dough into 60 (1-inch) balls. Place 2 inches apart on the prepared baking sheets. Flatten the cookies with the bottom of a glass. Sprinkle with 1 teaspoon granulated sugar. Bake at 375°F for 10 minutes or until golden brown. Cool 2 minutes on the baking sheets. Transfer to wire racks. Cool.

MAKE

You can easily make these gluten-free cookies ahead. Shape the dough into 1½-inch diameter logs, wrap in plastic wrap, and freeze. When you're ready to bake, thaw the dough for 20 minutes; cut into ½-inch-thick slices, and bake as directed.

CLASSIC SUGAR COOKIES

HANDS-ON: 25 minutes
TOTAL: 1 hour, 35 minutes
MAKES: 2 dozen cookies

- 8 ounces (1 cup) butter, softened
- 1 cup granulated sugar
- 1 large egg
- 1 teaspoon vanilla extract
- 3 cups (13.5 ounces) all-purpose flour
- ¼ teaspoon salt

Cooking spray

- 1 (16-ounce) package powdered sugar
- 6 tablespoons warm water

Liquid food coloring (optional)

1. Put the butter in a large bowl. Beat with an electric mixer at medium speed 2 minutes or until creamy. Gradually add the sugar, beating well. Add the egg and vanilla, beating well. Gradually add the flour and salt, beating until blended. Divide the dough in half; cover and chill 1 hour.

2. Preheat the oven to 350°F. Lightly grease baking sheets with the cooking spray. Roll each portion of the dough to ¼-inch thickness on a lightly floured surface. Cut with the desired cookie cutters. Place on the prepared baking sheets.

3. Bake at 350°F for 8 to 10 minutes or until the edges are lightly browned. Cool on the baking sheets 1 minute. Transfer to wire racks, and cool completely (about 20 minutes).

4. Stir together the powdered sugar and warm water using a wire whisk. Divide the mixture, and tint with food coloring, if desired.

EASY SANTA COOKIES

HANDS-ON: 1 hour
TOTAL: 2 hours
MAKES: 2 dozen cookies

- 1 (16.5-ounce) package refrigerated sugar cookie dough
- ¼ cup (1.1 ounces) all-purpose flour
- 2 cups powdered sugar
- 2 tablespoons butter, softened
- 2 to 3 tablespoons milk
- 2 to 3 drops red liquid food coloring
- 48 semisweet chocolate chips (about ¼ cup)
- 24 red cinnamon candies
- ⅔ cup flaked sweetened coconut
- 24 miniature marshmallows

Waxed paper

1. Break up the cookie dough into a medium bowl. Knead in the flour with your hands until well blended. Shape the dough into a log. If too soft to cut into slices, chill up to 30 minutes.

2. Preheat the oven to 350°F. Cut the dough into 24 (¼-inch) slices. Place the slices 3 inches apart on ungreased baking sheets. Bake at 350°F for 8 to 12 minutes or until golden brown. Cool on the baking sheets 2 minutes. Transfer to wire racks, and cool completely (about 20 minutes).

3. Stir together the powdered sugar, butter, and enough milk to make the frosting smooth and spreadable. Spoon half of the frosting into another small bowl. Add the red food coloring to the remaining frosting; stir until blended.

4. Frost the cookies with the red and white frosting. Use a small amount of frosting to attach the chocolate chips for eyes and cinnamon candy for the nose. Gently press the coconut into the white frosting for the beard. Press the marshmallow into the red frosting for the tassel of the cap. Put some white frosting in a zip-top plastic freezer bag. Snip 1 corner to make a small hole. Pipe white trim on Santa's cap. Let stand until the frosting is set. Store between sheets of waxed paper in a tightly covered container at room temperature.

BIG CRUNCHY SUGAR COOKIES

HANDS-ON: 20 minutes
TOTAL: 2 hours, 35 minutes
MAKES: 1½ dozen cookies

- 8 ounces (1 cup) unsalted butter, softened
- 1 cup granulated sugar
- 1 large egg
- 1½ teaspoons vanilla extract
- 2 cups (9 ounces) all-purpose flour
- ½ teaspoon baking powder
- ¼ teaspoon salt

Parchment paper

Assorted coarse sugar crystals

1. Put the butter in a large bowl. Beat with an electric mixer at medium speed until creamy. Gradually add 1 cup sugar, beating until smooth. Add the egg and vanilla, beating until blended.

2. Stir together the flour, baking powder, and salt; gradually add to the butter mixture, beating just until blended. Shape the dough into a ball; cover and chill 2 hours.

3. Preheat the oven to 375°F. Line baking sheets with the parchment paper. Divide the dough into 3 portions. Work with 1 portion of the dough at a time, storing the remaining dough in the refrigerator. Shape the dough into 1½-inch balls; roll each ball in the sugar crystals. Place 2 inches apart on the baking sheets. Gently press and flatten each ball of dough to ¾-inch thickness.

4. Bake at 375°F for 13 to 15 minutes or until the edges of the cookies are lightly browned. Cool 5 minutes on baking sheets. Transfer to wire racks. Cool.

CHOCOLATE CHIP REINDEER COOKIES

HANDS-ON: 1 hour, 15 minutes
TOTAL: 4 hours, 30 minutes
MAKES: 16 cookies

- 1 (17.5-ounce) pouch chocolate chip cookie mix
- 1 tablespoon all-purpose flour
- 4 ounces (½ cup) butter, softened
- 1 large egg
- 2 (7-ounce) pouches chocolate flavored cookie decorating icing
- 32 candy eyes
- 16 small round chocolate-covered creamy mints
- 1 (7-ounce) pouch white cookie decorating icing

1. Put the first 4 ingredients in a large bowl. Beat with an electric mixer at low speed just until blended. Shape into a ball. Flatten dough to ½-inch thickness; wrap in plastic wrap. Chill 3 hours or until very firm.

2. Preheat the oven to 350°F. Unwrap the dough. Place on a well-floured surface; roll the dough to ¼-inch thickness. Cut with a floured 3½-inch gingerbread boy cookie cutter. Place cutouts 2 inches apart on ungreased baking sheets. Chill on the baking sheets 10 minutes. Bake at 350°F for 9 to 10 minutes or until the edges are light golden brown. Transfer to wire racks, and cool completely (about 20 minutes).

3. Turn each cookie upside down to look like a reindeer face. Outline each cookie with chocolate icing; fill in, and spread icing with a wooden pick. Attach the candy eyes and a mint for the nose. Add antlers using the white icing. Let stand until set.

ICED BROWNED BUTTER SUGAR COOKIES

- -

HANDS-ON: 45 minutes
TOTAL: 1 hour
MAKES: 32 cookies

Parchment paper
4.5 ounces (⅔ cup) unsalted butter
 1 cup granulated sugar
 ¾ teaspoon vanilla extract
 3 large egg yolks
1¾ cups (8 ounces) all-purpose flour
 ½ teaspoon salt
 ¼ teaspoon baking powder

Waxed paper
 1 cup powdered sugar
1½ tablespoons half-and-half
 ⅓ cup pearlized sugar or turbinado
     sugar

1. Preheat oven to 350°F. Line baking sheets with parchment paper.

2. Melt butter in a large skillet over medium-low heat; cook 6 minutes or until dark brown. Pour butter into a large bowl; let stand 5 minutes. Add granulated sugar and ½ teaspoon vanilla. Beat with an electric mixer at medium speed until well blended (about 2 minutes). Add egg yolks, and beat at medium speed until well blended (about 1 minute).

3. Stir together flour, salt, and baking powder with a whisk. Add flour mixture to butter mixture; beat at low speed just until combined. Turn dough out onto a sheet of waxed paper; knead gently 7 times with hands. Roll dough to a ¼-inch thickness. Cut with a 2½-inch star-shaped cookie cutter into 32 cookies; reroll scraps as necessary. Arrange cookies 1 inch apart on prepared baking sheets. Bake, 1 batch at a time, at 350°F for 10 minutes or until edges are lightly browned. Transfer cookies to wire racks. Cool completely.

4. Stir together powdered sugar, half-and-half, and remaining ¼ teaspoon vanilla with a whisk until icing is smooth. Spoon about ¾ teaspoon icing onto each cookie; spread to edges. While icing is wet, sprinkle each cookie with ½ teaspoon pearlized sugar. Let stand on wire racks until dry.

MR. & MRS. CLAUS COOKIES

HANDS-ON: 2 hours, 10 minutes
TOTAL: 3 hours
MAKES: 1 dozen cookies

1 (16-ounce) package refrigerated sugar cookie dough

¼ cup (1.1 ounces) all-purpose flour

2 (7-ounce) pouches red cookie decorating icing

1 (7-ounce) pouch white cookie decorating icing

1 (7-ounce) pouch black cookie decorating icing

White sanding sugar

6 miniature marshmallows

½ cup miniature marshmallow bits

Black string licorice, cut into 2½-inch pieces or black cookie icing

Silver candy sprinkles

Pink, black, and white confetti

Holly and berry candy sprinkles

1. Preheat the oven to 350°F. Crumble the cookie dough in a large bowl. Knead in the flour with your hands until well blended.

2. Place the dough on a floured surface; roll to ⅛-inch thickness. Cut with 5-inch Santa and Mrs. Claus cookie cutters. Place the cutouts 1 inch apart on ungreased baking sheets. Chill 10 minutes.

3. Bake at 350°F for 10 to 12 minutes or until lightly browned. Immediately transfer from the baking sheets to wire racks. Cool completely.

4. Frost and decorate Santa and Mrs. Claus cookies with the red, white, and black icing. Sprinkle the sugar on Mrs. Claus for hair. Cut 6 miniature marshmallows in half; arrange on Santa cookies for the pom-pom and Mrs. Claus for her bun. Use white icing to attach marshmallow bits for beard. Press the licorice into the Santa cookies for the belt; use black icing to attach sprinkles for the buckle. Decorate with the confetti and the holly and berry sprinkles.

FESTIVE ORNAMENT COOKIES

HANDS-ON: 15 minutes
TOTAL: 45 minutes
MAKES: 20 cookies

1 (16.5-ounce) package refrigerated sugar cookie dough

¼ cup (1.1 ounces) all-purpose flour

1 (7-ounce) pouch red cookie decorating icing

1 (7-ounce) pouch green cookie decorating icing

1 (7-ounce) pouch white cookie decorating icing

¼ cup red and green miniature candy-coated chocolate candies

1. Preheat the oven to 350°F. Break up the cookie dough into a medium bowl. Knead in the flour with your hands until well blended.

2. Place the dough on a lightly floured surface, and roll to ¼-inch thickness. Cut with a floured 3- to 3½-inch ornament-shaped cookie cutter. Place 2 inches apart on ungreased baking sheets.

3. Bake at 350°F for 10 to 12 minutes or until set and the edges are lightly browned. Cool on baking sheets 2 minutes. Transfer to wire racks, and cool completely (about 20 minutes).

4. Spread the tops of the cookies with your desired color of cookie icing, and pipe the preferred designs. Add the candies as desired for decorations.

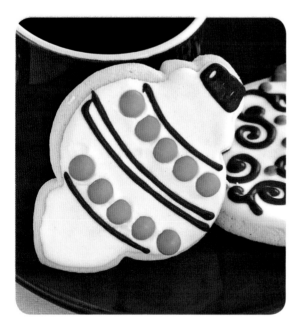

FROSTED SUGAR 'N' SPICE COOKIES

HANDS-ON: 1 hour, 10 minutes
TOTAL: 3 hours, 43 minutes
MAKES: 2½ dozen cookies

Cookies:

2 cups (9 ounces) all-purpose flour

1 teaspoon baking powder

½ teaspoon baking soda

½ teaspoon ground cinnamon

¼ teaspoon salt

⅛ teaspoon ground nutmeg

2½ ounces (⅓ cup) butter, softened

½ cup granulated sugar

½ cup firmly packed brown sugar

2 large egg yolks

5 ounces cream cheese, softened

1 teaspoon grated orange zest

1 teaspoon vanilla extract

Simple White Frosting:

2 ounces (¼ cup) butter, softened

⅛ teaspoon salt

3 cups powdered sugar

4 tablespoons milk

Yellow sparkling sugar

1. **Make the cookies:** Stir together the first 6 ingredients in a bowl.

2. Put the butter and the next 3 ingredients in a large bowl. Beat with an electric mixer at medium speed until creamy. Add the cream cheese, orange zest, and vanilla; beat until well blended. Gradually add the flour mixture, beating at low speed until blended.

3. Divide the dough in half, shaping into 2 flattened disks. Cover the dough

disks with plastic wrap, and chill 2 to 24 hours.

4. Preheat the oven to 350°F. Place 1 dough disk on a floured surface. Roll to ¼-inch thickness; cut with a 4-inch star-shaped cutter. Place 1 inch apart on ungreased baking sheets. Repeat the procedure with the remaining dough disk.

5. Bake at 350°F for 8 to 10 minutes or just until the edges are lightly browned. Cool on baking sheets 3 minutes. Transfer to a wire rack, and cool completely (about 30 minutes).

6. **Make the frosting:** Put the butter, ⅛ teaspoon salt, 1½ cups powdered sugar, and 3 tablespoons milk in a large bowl. Beat with an electric mixer at medium speed until blended. Gradually beat in the remaining powdered sugar and milk.

7. Spread the cookies with a thin layer of Simple White Frosting, and top with the colored sugar.

ICED GINGERBREAD BISCOTTI

HANDS-ON: 30 minutes
TOTAL: 1 hour, 50 minutes
MAKES: 22 biscotti

Biscotti:

Parchment paper

- 1 cup granulated sugar
- 2 tablespoons molasses
- 2 teaspoons vanilla extract
- 3 large eggs
- 1¼ cups (5.3 ounces) whole-wheat pastry flour
- 1 cup plus 3 tablespoons (5.3 ounces) all-purpose flour
- 1½ teaspoons ground cinnamon
- 1 teaspoon ground ginger
- ½ teaspoon salt
- ½ teaspoon ground cloves
- ½ teaspoon baking powder

Icing:

- ⅔ cup powdered sugar
- 1 tablespoon whole milk
- ¼ teaspoon vanilla extract

1. Preheat the oven to 325°F. Line a baking sheet with the parchment paper.

2. Make the biscotti: Put the granulated sugar, molasses, 2 teaspoons vanilla, and 2 eggs in the bowl of a heavy-duty electric stand mixer. Beat at high speed until batter falls in ribbons when beaters are lifted (about 6 minutes).

3. Stir together the flours and next 5 ingredients in a bowl with a whisk. Add the flour mixture to the egg mixture; beat at low speed just until combined. Divide the dough in half; place the halves on the prepared baking sheet. Shape each half into an 8- x 4-inch loaf with lightly floured hands. Lightly beat remaining egg in a bowl; brush the tops and sides of the loaves with the egg. Bake at 325°F for 35 minutes or until golden brown. Transfer the loaves to a wire rack, and cool 10 minutes.

4. Reduce oven temperature to 275°F.

5. Cut each loaf diagonally into 11 (½-inch) slices; place the slices, cut sides down, on the baking sheet. Bake at 275°F for 20 minutes, turning the slices over after 10 minutes. Transfer to a wire rack, and cool completely.

6. Make the icing: Stir together the powdered sugar, milk, and ¼ teaspoon vanilla with a whisk until smooth. Drizzle the icing over the biscotti; let stand until icing sets. Store the cookies in an airtight container.

PAPER DOLL GINGERBREAD GIRLS

HANDS-ON: 1 hour
TOTAL: 2 hours, 10 minutes
MAKES: 1 dozen cookies

1 (17.5-ounce) pouch gingerbread cookie mix

4 ounces (½ cup) butter, softened

1 tablespoon water

1 large egg

1 (7-ounce) pouch white cookie decorating icing

1 (7-ounce) pouch red cookie decorating icing

Hot pink decorator sugar crystals

Lime-green sanding sugar

Pink and white edible decorating confetti

2 rolls strawberry chewy fruit snack (from a 5-ounce box)

Miniature red candy-coated chocolate candies

Snowflake candy sprinkles

Assorted holiday candy sprinkles

Lime-green round candies

1. Preheat the oven to 350°F. Stir together the cookie mix, butter, 1 tablespoon water, and egg until a soft dough forms.

2. Place the dough on a floured surface, and roll to ¼-inch thickness. Cut with a floured 5-inch gingerbread girl cookie cutter. Place the cutouts 2 inches apart on ungreased baking sheets.

3. Bake at 350°F for 8 to 10 minutes or until the edges are set. Cool 1 minute. Transfer to wire racks, and cool completely (about 20 minutes). Pipe the icing onto the cookies in desired design. Decorate with the sugar crystals and candies.

SNOW GLOBE COOKIES

Hands-on: 30 minutes
Total: 1 hour, 30 minutes
Makes: 8 to 10 cookies

Cookies:

- 6 ounces (¾ cup) butter, softened
- ¾ cup firmly packed light brown sugar
- ¾ cup molasses
- ¼ teaspoon salt
- 2 teaspoons ground cinnamon
- 2 teaspoons ground ginger
- ¼ teaspoon ground allspice
- ¼ teaspoon ground cardamom
- 1 large egg
- 3½ cups (15.75 ounces) all-purpose flour
- 1 teaspoon baking powder
- ½ teaspoon baking soda

Parchment paper

Royal Icing:

- 1 (32-ounce) package powdered sugar (about 7½ cups)
- 4 teaspoons meringue powder
- 10 to 12 tablespoons warm water

Blue, green, red, and yellow food coloring paste

White nonpareils, yellow stars, and red sanding sugar

1. Make the cookies: Melt the butter in a heavy saucepan over low heat; whisk in the brown sugar and next 6 ingredients. Put mixture in the bowl of a heavy-duty electric stand mixer; let stand 30 minutes. Add the egg, beating just until blended.

2. Stir together the flour, baking powder, and baking soda in a medium bowl; gradually add to the butter mixture, beating at a low speed just until blended.

3. Preheat the oven to 350°F. Line baking sheets with the parchment paper. Place the dough on a lightly floured surface, and roll to a ¼-inch thickness. Cut 8 to 10 cookies with a 4-inch snow globe cutter, reserving the remaining dough. Place the cookies 1 inch apart on the prepared baking sheets. Create other desired shapes, like mini gingerbread men, snowmen, and trees, using mini cutters and the remaining dough. Place the shapes 1 inch apart on a second prepared baking sheet.

4. Bake the snow globe cookies at 350°F for 10 to 12 minutes or until lightly browned. Let stand 5 minutes. Transfer to wire racks, and cool completely (about 20 minutes). Bake the gingerbread men, snowmen, and tree cookies for 6 to 8 minutes or until lightly browned. Let stand 5 minutes. Transfer to wire racks, and cool completely (about 20 minutes).

5. **Make the icing:** Beat the powdered sugar, meringue powder, and 10 tablespoons warm water with an electric mixer at low speed until blended. Add up to 2 tablespoons more water, 1 teaspoon at a time, until desired consistency is reached. Separate the icing into 5 bowls. Add the blue, green, red, and yellow food coloring to each of 4 bowls, one color to each bowl. Place the icing into each of 5 zip-top plastic bags.

6. Snip one corner of each icing bag to create a small hole. Decorate the cookies in stages, using the white icing first to create the snow. Add the white nonpareils, and let stand 10 minutes. Fill in the background with the blue icing, and place the gingerbread men or the tree cookies on top, while the icing is still wet. Sprinkle the white nonpareils for the falling snow effect; let stand 10 minutes. Add the red icing to create the base. Let the decorated cookies harden for 1 hour.

SILVER BELLS

HANDS-ON: 15 minutes
TOTAL: 1 hour, 10 minutes
MAKES: 2½ dozen cookies

1 (16.5-ounce) package refrigerated sugar cookie dough

¼ cup (1.1 ounces) all-purpose flour

2 (7-ounce) pouches white cookie decorating icing

½ cup silver sanding sugar

TIP: Feel free to decorate with any colored sanding sugar.

1. Preheat the oven to 350°F. Break up the cookie dough into a medium bowl. Add the flour, and knead with your hands until well blended.

2. Place the dough on a lightly floured surface, and roll to ¼-inch thickness. Cut with a floured 3¾-inch bell-shaped cookie cutter. Place 2 inches apart on ungreased baking sheets. Reroll the dough, and cut additional cookies.

3. Bake at 350°F for 10 to 12 minutes or until the edges are lightly browned. Cool on the baking sheets 5 minutes. Transfer to wire racks, and cool completely (about 20 minutes).

4. Spread tops of cookies with the white icing; sprinkle with the sanding sugar. Let stand until set.

CHRISTMAS WREATH COOKIES

HANDS-ON: 20 minutes
TOTAL: 1 hour, 40 minutes
MAKES: 2 dozen cookies

- 1 (16.5-ounce) package refrigerated sugar cookie dough
- ¼ cup (1.1 ounces) all-purpose flour
- ¼ teaspoon green food coloring paste
- ½ cup sweetened dried cranberries, chopped
- 1 (4.25-ounce) tube red cookie decorating icing
- 24 red candy-coated chocolate candies

1. Break up the cookie dough into a bowl. Knead in the flour and food coloring with your hands until blended. Stir in the cranberries. Wrap the dough in plastic wrap; chill 1 hour.

2. Preheat the oven to 350°F. Unwrap the dough; divide into 24 portions. Roll each portion into a 5-inch log. Gently shape each log into a wreath, pressing the ends together. Place cookies about 2 inches apart on ungreased baking sheets.

3. Bake at 350°F for 10 to 12 minutes or until set. Cool on baking sheets 2 minutes. Transfer to wire racks, and cool completely (about 20 minutes).

4. With decorating icing, pipe a small bow at the seam of each cookie; place chocolate candies in the center of each bow.

NO-BAKE WREATH COOKIES

HANDS-ON: 10 minutes
TOTAL: 40 minutes
MAKES: 20 cookies

1 (16-ounce) bag green candy melts or coating wafers

2½ cups coarsely crushed bite-size shredded whole-wheat cereal biscuits

Waxed paper

¼ cup miniature candy-coated chocolate candies

1. Place the candy melts in a medium microwave-safe bowl; microwave at MEDIUM 1 minute 30 seconds, stirring at 30-second intervals. Add the cereal; stir gently to coat.

2. Drop the cereal mixture by heaping tablespoonfuls onto the waxed paper; shape each spoonful into a wreath. Decorate with the candies. Let stand about 30 minutes or until set.

STRAWBERRY ROCKY ROAD CANDY, PAGE 96

GIFTABLE GOODIES

- -

make everyone on your list feel extra-special with these homemade treats!

STRAWBERRY ROCKY ROAD CANDY

HANDS-ON: 15 minutes
TOTAL: 15 minutes
MAKES: about 32 pieces

Waxed paper

Cooking spray

- 4 cups semisweet chocolate chips (24 ounces)
- 3 cups miniature marshmallows
- 2 cups chopped dried strawberries
- 1 cup blanched whole almonds, coarsely chopped

TIP: This simple candy will look elegant in clear plastic bags wrapped with a decorative red ribbon. Be sure to place pieces of parchment in between the candy pieces.

1. Line a 15- x 10-inch rimmed baking sheet with waxed paper; spray the paper with cooking spray. Fill a 3-quart saucepan half full with water; heat to simmering. Put the chocolate chips in a 2-quart heatproof bowl; place the bowl over pan of simmering water. Cook 4 to 5 minutes or until melted and the chips can be stirred smooth. Remove from heat. Stir in the marshmallows just until blended.

2. Spread mixture in prepared pan. Sprinkle with the strawberries and almonds; press gently to adhere to chocolate. Chill 1 hour or until set. Break the candy into 32 irregular pieces. Store in refrigerator.

WHITE CHOCOLATE-PEPPERMINT JUMBLES

HANDS-ON: 15 minutes
TOTAL: 2 hours, 45 minutes
MAKES: about 8 dozen jumbles

- 2 (16-ounce) packages vanilla-flavored candy coating (almond bark)
- 1 (12-ounce) bag white vanilla baking chips (2 cups)
- 6 ounces white chocolate, chopped
- 3 tablespoons shortening
- 1 (16-ounce) package pretzel nuggets
- 1 (8-ounce) package animal-shaped cookies (3 cups)
- 1 cup coarsely crushed hard peppermint candy

Waxed paper

1. Put the candy coating, vanilla chips, white chocolate, and shortening in a 6-quart electric slow cooker. Cover; cook on LOW 1 hour and 30 minutes or until the candy coating and white chocolate look very soft. Stir until smooth. Stir in the pretzels, cookies, and crushed peppermint candy.

2. Drop the candy by heaping tablespoonfuls onto the waxed paper. Let stand 1 hour or until firm.

PUMPKIN-SPICE COOKIE GRANOLA

HANDS-ON: 35 minutes
TOTAL: 1 hour, 15 minutes
MAKES: 23 pieces

Aluminum foil

- 1 **(16.5-ounce) roll refrigerated sugar cookie dough**
- ½ **teaspoon pumpkin pie spice**
- 2½ **cups old-fashioned oats**
- 1 **cup roasted salted hulled pumpkin seeds (pepitas)**
- 1 **cup chopped pecans**
- 1 **cup pistachios**
- ⅔ **cup sweetened dried cranberries**
- 1 **cup white vanilla baking chips (6 ounces)**

TIP: Package the granola in ½-cup amounts in small zip-top storage bags for handy serving-size snacking. Or package in decorative containers for gift-giving.

1. Preheat the oven to 325°F. Line 2 large rimmed baking sheets with the aluminum foil. Let the cookie dough stand at room temperature 10 minutes to soften.

2. Stir together the cookie dough and pumpkin pie spice in a large bowl. Add the oats, pumpkin seeds, pecans, and pistachios; knead into the dough until well blended. Crumble the mixture evenly onto prepared baking sheets.

3. Bake 325°F for 17 to 22 minutes, stirring every 5 minutes and rotating the baking sheets halfway through baking, until light golden brown. Cool completely on the baking sheets, (about 30 minutes).

4. Break the granola into smaller pieces, if necessary. Stir together the granola, cranberries, and white chips in a large bowl. Store tightly covered at room temperature.

COCONUT-ALMOND TRUFFLES

HANDS-ON: 25 minutes
TOTAL: 40 minutes
MAKES: 16 truffles

Parchment paper

- 1 (8-ounce) can almond paste
- ¾ cup flaked sweetened coconut, toasted
- 1½ cups chopped almonds
- ¼ teaspoon coconut extract
- 8 ounces bittersweet chocolate
- 1 tablespoon shortening

1. Line a baking sheet with the parchment paper. Put the almond paste, ½ cup coconut, almonds, and coconut extract in a food processor. Cover; process with on-and-off pulses 3 or 4 times or until combined. (Mixture will be crumbly.) Shape the dough into 16 (1-inch) balls.

2. Put the chocolate and shortening in a 4-cup microwave-safe measuring cup; microwave, uncovered, at HIGH 1 minute 30 seconds to 2 minutes, stirring at 30-second intervals, until melted and smooth. Dip the balls into the chocolate. Place on the prepared baking sheet. Immediately sprinkle the tops with remaining ¼ cup coconut. Chill until firm (about 15 minutes). Store tightly covered in refrigerator up to 2 weeks.

TIP: To toast coconut, sprinkle in an ungreased skillet. Cook over medium-low heat 6 to 14 minutes, stirring frequently until browning begins, and then stirring constantly until golden brown.

CANDY CANE BISCOTTI

HANDS-ON: 14 minutes
TOTAL: 2 hours, 30 minutes
MAKES: about 2½ dozen biscotti

- ¾ cup granulated sugar
- 8 ounces (1 cup) butter, softened
- 2 large eggs, lightly beaten
- 2½ cups (11.25 ounces) all-purpose flour
- 2 teaspoons baking powder
- ¼ teaspoon salt
- 1 tablespoon peppermint schnapps
- 1 teaspoon vanilla extract
- ¾ cup crushed soft peppermint sticks
- Waxed paper
- 4 ounces dark chocolate, chopped
- Coarse sugar

1. Preheat the oven to 350°F. Put the sugar and butter in a large bowl. Beat with an electric mixer at medium speed until creamy. Add the eggs, 1 at a time, beating until blended after each addition. Stir together the flour, baking powder, and salt; gradually add to the butter mixture, beating until blended. Stir in the peppermint schnapps and vanilla. Stir in ½ cup of the crushed peppermint.

2. Divide the dough in half. Shape each portion of the dough into a 9- x 2-inch log on a prepared baking sheet, using lightly floured hands.

3. Bake at 350°F for 28 to 30 minutes or until firm. Transfer to wire racks; cool completely (about 1 hour). Cut each log diagonally into ½-inch-thick slices with a serrated knife, using a gentle sawing motion. Place the slices, cut sides down, on the baking sheets.

4. Bake at 350°F for 10 minutes; turn the cookies over, and bake 8 more minutes. Transfer to wire racks set over waxed paper, and cool completely (about 30 minutes).

5. Put the chocolate in a small microwave-safe bowl; microwave at HIGH 30 to 60 seconds or until melted and smooth, stirring at 30-second intervals. Drizzle the chocolate over tops of the biscotti; sprinkle with coarse sugar and the remaining ¼ cup crushed peppermint. Let stand until chocolate is set.

TROPICAL WHITE CHOCOLATE FUDGE

HANDS-ON: 21 minutes
TOTAL: 2 hours, 21 minutes
MAKES: 64 pieces

Aluminum foil

Cooking spray

4 ounces (½ cup) butter

2 cups granulated sugar

¾ cup sour cream

12 ounces white chocolate, chopped

1 (7-ounce) jar marshmallow creme

½ cup dried apricots, chopped

½ cup dried pineapple, chopped

¾ cup chopped macadamia nuts

½ cup flaked sweetened coconut, toasted

TIP: Visit your local craft store to select the perfect holiday tin to package this fudge.

1. Line the bottom and sides of a 9-inch square pan with aluminum foil, allowing 2 to 3 inches to extend over sides; lightly spray the foil with cooking spray.

2. Combine the butter, sugar, and sour cream in a large heavy saucepan over medium heat. Bring to a boil; cook, stirring constantly, to 234°F on a candy thermometer or until a small amount of the mixture dropped into a cup of very cold water forms a ball that flattens when removed from the water, about 5 minutes.

3. Remove from the heat; stir in the chocolate and marshmallow creme until melted. Fold in the dried fruit and macadamia nuts; quickly pour into prepared pan, spreading evenly. Sprinkle the coconut over top, pressing gently. Cool completely in the pan (about 2 hours). Lift the fudge from the pan, using the foil sides as handles. Gently remove the foil. Cut the fudge into 8 rows by 8 rows.

RED VELVET MOON PIES

HANDS-ON: 35 minutes
TOTAL: 1 hour, 5 minutes
MAKES: 18 moon pies

Cookies:
Parchment paper

2¾ cups (12.4 ounces) all-purpose flour

⅓ cup unsweetened cocoa

1½ teaspoons baking powder

½ teaspoon baking soda

¼ teaspoon salt

8 ounces (1 cup) butter, softened

1¼ cups granulated sugar

2 large eggs

2 tablespoons red liquid food coloring

1 tablespoon vanilla extract

¾ cup buttermilk

Marshmallow Filling:

8 ounces (½ cup) butter, softened

1 cup sifted powdered sugar

1 cup marshmallow creme

½ teaspoon vanilla extract

1. Make the cookies: Preheat the oven to 350°F. Line baking sheets with the parchment paper. Stir together the flour and next 4 ingredients in a medium bowl.

2. Put the butter in a large bowl. Beat with an electric mixer at medium speed 2 minutes or until creamy. Gradually add the sugar, beating well. Add the eggs, 1 at a time, beating until blended after each addition. Beat in the food coloring and vanilla.

3. Add the flour mixture alternately with the buttermilk, beginning and ending with the flour mixture. Beat at low speed until blended after each addition, stopping to scrape the bowl as needed.

4. Drop the dough by tablespoonfuls onto prepared baking sheets. Spread the dough to 2-inch rounds.

5. Bake at 350°F for 15 minutes or until tops are set. Cool on the baking sheets 5 minutes. Transfer to wire racks, and cool completely (about 20 minutes).

6. Make the filling: Put the butter in a bowl. Beat with an electric mixer at medium speed until creamy; gradually add sugar, beating well. Add remaining ingredients, beating until well blended. Spread the filling onto the center of 18 cookie bottoms. Top with the remaining cookies, bottom sides down, gently pressing together.

SUGAR COOKIE MACAROONS

HANDS-ON: 25 minutes
TOTAL: 1 hour, 10 minutes
MAKES: 40 cookies

Shortening or cooking spray

1 (16-ounce) package ready-to-bake sugar cookies

3 cups flaked sweetened coconut

4 ounces bittersweet chocolate, chopped

2 tablespoons whipping cream

1. Preheat the oven to 350°F. Lightly grease baking sheets with shortening or cooking spray. Cut each cookie dough portion into 4 equal pieces (to make 80 total). Roll the dough pieces in the coconut; shape into balls. Place the balls 2 inches apart on the prepared baking sheets.

2. Bake at 350°F for 12 to 13 minutes or until the edges are golden. Cool 5 minutes. Transfer to wire racks. Cool completely.

3. Put the chocolate and whipping cream in a small microwave-safe bowl; microwave, uncovered, at HIGH 30 seconds; stir. Spoon mixture into a small zip-top plastic freezer bag. Cut off a tiny corner of the bag. Squeeze the bag to pipe ½ to 1 teaspoon of the chocolate mixture onto the center of 40 cookie bottoms. Top with the remaining cookies, bottom sides down, gently pressing together. Let stand on wire racks 30 minutes or until set.

PRALINE PECANS

HANDS-ON: 15 minutes
TOTAL: 35 minutes
MAKES: about 32 pieces

Waxed paper

- 1½ cups granulated sugar
- ¾ cup packed brown sugar
- 4 ounces (½ cup) butter, cut into pieces
- ½ cup milk
- 2 tablespoons corn syrup
- 5 cups pecan halves, toasted

1. Line a 15- x 10-inch rimmed baking sheet with waxed paper. Stir together the granulated sugar, brown sugar, butter, milk, and corn syrup in a heavy 3-quart saucepan. Heat to boiling over medium heat, stirring constantly. Boil 7 to 8 minutes, stirring constantly, to 234°F on a candy thermometer or until a small amount of the mixture dropped into a cup of very cold water forms a ball that flattens when removed from the water.

2. Remove from the heat; vigorously stir in the pecans. Spoon the mixture into the prepared pan, spreading in an even layer. Let stand 20 minutes or until firm. Break into pieces. Store in an airtight container at room temperature up to 1 week.

SALTY CHOCOLATE-PECAN CANDY

HANDS-ON: 20 minutes
TOTAL: 1 hour, 20 minutes
MAKES: about 30 pieces

1 cup pecans, coarsely chopped

Parchment paper

4 ounces bittersweet chocolate baking bars

4 ounces white chocolate baking bars

1 teaspoon coarse sea salt

TIP: Wrap this yummy candy in a box lined with parchment and a bow. It will definitely be one of the best gifts under the tree!

1. Preheat the oven to 350°F. Spread the pecans in an ungreased shallow pan. Bake, uncovered, at 350°F for 6 to 10 minutes, stirring occasionally, until light brown. Remove from the oven. Reduce the oven temperature to 225°F.

2. Line a 17- x 12-inch half-sheet pan with the parchment paper. Break each baking bar into 8 equal pieces. Arrange in a checkerboard pattern in the pan, alternating bittersweet and white chocolate. (Pieces will touch.)

3. Bake at 225°F for 5 minutes or just until chocolate is melted. Place pan on a wire rack. Swirl with a knife for marbled design. Sprinkle evenly with the toasted pecans and salt.

4. Chill 1 hour or until firm. Break into pieces. Store in an airtight container in the refrigerator up to 1 month.

FUDGY BROWNIE BITES

HANDS-ON: 15 minutes
TOTAL: 1 hour
MAKES: about 38 brownie bites

- 38 mini paper baking cups
- 1 tablespoon instant espresso powder
- ¼ cup hot water
- ½ cup vegetable or canola oil
- 2 large eggs
- 1 (1-pound, 2.3-ounce) box fudge brownie mix
- 1 cup semisweet chocolate chips (6 ounces)
- 1 cup coarsely chopped walnuts

1. Preheat the oven to 375°F. Place 1 mini paper baking cup in each of 38 mini muffin cups.

2. Dissolve coffee powder in hot water in a 2-cup glass measuring cup, stirring with a small whisk. Cool slightly. Stir in the oil and eggs with a whisk until blended.

3. Put the brownie mix in a large bowl; break up the large lumps with the back of a spoon. Stir in the coffee mixture until blended. Stir in the chocolate chips and walnuts. Spoon the mixture into muffin cups, filling full.

4. Bake at 375°F for 12 to 14 minutes or until the tops are shiny and crusty and the centers are set. Cool completely in pans on wire racks (about 30 minutes). Remove from pans.

CARDAMOM SUGAR THINS

HANDS-ON: 2 hours
TOTAL: 2 hours, 10 minutes
MAKES: about 5 dozen cookies

- 2 cups (9 ounces) all-purpose flour
- 1 teaspoon ground cardamom
- ½ teaspoon baking powder
- ¼ teaspoon salt
- 4 ounces (½ cup) butter, softened
- 1 cup granulated sugar
- 1 large egg
- 1 large egg yolk
- 1 teaspoon vanilla extract

Waxed paper or parchment paper

Powdered sugar

1. Stir together the flour, cardamom, baking powder, and salt in medium bowl until blended. Put the butter and granulated sugar in a large bowl. Beat with an electric mixer at medium speed 3 minutes or until light and fluffy. Add the egg, egg yolk, and vanilla; beat at low speed until combined. Add the flour mixture; beat until a soft dough forms. Cover; chill 10 to 15 minutes or until firm.

2. Preheat the oven to 350°F. Place half the dough on a lightly floured surface, or between 2 sheets of waxed paper or parchment paper. Roll to ⅛-inch thickness. Using a 2-inch scalloped cookie cutter, cut out the dough, rerolling scraps as necessary. Place cutouts 1½ inches apart on ungreased baking sheets. Repeat with the remaining half of dough.

3. Bake at 350°F for 8 to 10 minutes or until edges are light brown. Cool 2 minutes. Transfer to wire racks. Sprinkle with the powdered sugar. Cool completely before storing in an airtight container at room temperature.

MAKE

To form diamond shapes, use a knife instead of a cookie cutter. Cut the dough into 2-inch strips, and then cut the strips diagonally. For a ruffled edge, use a pastry wheel instead of a knife.

PEPPERMINT-PINWHEEL COOKIES

HANDS-ON: 40 minutes
TOTAL: 5 hours
MAKES: 4 dozen cookies

Cookies:
- 4 ounces (½ cup) butter, softened
- 1 cup granulated sugar
- 1 large egg
- ½ teaspoon vanilla extract
- 1¾ cups (7.9 ounces) all-purpose flour
- ½ teaspoon baking soda
- ¼ teaspoon salt

Plastic wrap
- ¾ teaspoon red food coloring paste

Parchment paper

Peppermint Frosting:
- 2 ounces (¼ cup) butter, softened
- 1 (3-ounce) package cream cheese, softened
- 2 cups powdered sugar
- 1 tablespoon milk
- ⅛ teaspoon peppermint extract

1. Make the cookies: Put the butter in the bowl of a heavy-duty electric stand mixer. Beat at medium speed until creamy; gradually add the sugar, beating until light and fluffy. Add the egg and vanilla, beating until blended, scraping bowl as needed.

2. Stir together the flour, baking soda, and salt; gradually add the flour mixture to the butter mixture, beating at low speed until blended after each addition.

3. Divide the dough into 2 equal portions. Roll 1 portion of the dough into a 12- x 8-inch rectangle on a piece of lightly floured plastic wrap.

4. Knead the food coloring paste into the remaining portion of the dough while wearing rubber gloves. Roll the tinted dough into a rectangle as directed in Step 3. Invert the untinted dough onto the tinted dough; peel off the top piece of plastic wrap. Cut the dough in half lengthwise, forming 2 (12- x 4-inch) rectangles. Roll up each rectangle, jelly-roll fashion, starting at 1 long side and using the bottom piece of plastic wrap as a guide. Wrap the dough log in plastic wrap, and freeze 4 hours or up to 1 month.

5. Preheat the oven to 350°F. Line baking sheets with the parchment paper. Cut the ends off each dough log, and discard. Cut the dough into ¼-inch-thick pieces, and place on the prepared baking sheets.

6. Bake at 350°F for 6 to 7 minutes or until puffed and set; cool the cookies on the baking sheets 5 minutes. Transfer to wire racks, and cool completely.

7. **Make the frosting:** Put the butter and cream cheese in a bowl. Beat with an electric mixer at medium speed until creamy. Gradually add the powdered sugar, beating at low speed until blended. Increase speed to medium, and gradually add the milk and peppermint extract, beating until smooth.

8. Put the frosting in a zip-top plastic freezer bag. Snip 1 corner of the bag to make a small hole. Pipe about 2 teaspoons of the frosting onto half of the cookies; top with the remaining cookies, gently pressing to form a sandwich.

WHITE HEAVENLY HASH

HANDS-ON: 10 minutes
TOTAL: 35 minutes
MAKES: about 32 pieces

Waxed paper
- ¾ **cup granulated sugar**
- ¾ **cup whipping cream**
- 2 **tablespoons light corn syrup**
- 1 **(12-ounce) bag white vanilla baking chips (2 cups)**
- 1½ **cups miniature marshmallows**
- 1 **cup flaked sweetened coconut**
- 1 **cup chopped macadamia nuts**

TIP: This pretty candy looks like a winter snowflake. Wrap it in clear plastic bags and tie with a sparkly silver ribbon.

1. Line 2 baking sheets with the waxed paper. Stir together the sugar, whipping cream, and corn syrup in a 4-quart heavy saucepan; cook over medium-low heat, stirring frequently, until the sugar is dissolved. Heat to boiling over medium heat; cook about 6 minutes, without stirring, to 234°F on a candy thermometer or until a small amount of the mixture dropped into a cup of very cold water forms a soft ball that flattens when removed from the water. Remove from the heat. Add the baking chips; stir until smooth.

2. Gently stir in the marshmallows, coconut, and nuts. Drop the mixture by 2 tablespoonfuls onto the prepared baking sheets. Let stand until firm.

VIENNESE ALMOND CRESCENTS

Hands-on: 15 minutes
Total: 40 minutes
Makes: about 40 cookies

Parchment paper

- 1⅔ cups (7.5 ounces) all-purpose flour
- ⅔ cup almond meal
- ¼ teaspoon kosher salt
- 8 ounces (1 cup) butter, softened
- ⅓ cup granulated sugar
- 1 cup powdered sugar

1. Preheat the oven to 350°F. Line 2 large baking sheets with the parchment paper.

2. Stir together the flour, almond meal, and salt in a small bowl with a wire whisk. Put the butter and granulated sugar in a large bowl. Beat with an electric mixer at medium speed until light and fluffy, about 4 minutes. Gradually add the flour mixture to the butter mixture, beating until blended. Chill 10 minutes.

3. Shape the dough into 40 (2-inch) logs; bend the logs to form crescent shapes. Place the crescents 2 inches apart on the prepared baking sheets. Bake at 350°F for 12 minutes or until the edges are light golden brown. Transfer to wire racks, and cool completely (about 20 minutes). Sprinkle the cooled cookies with powdered sugar.

PISTACHIO PASTRY TWISTS

HANDS-ON: 20 minutes
TOTAL: 40 minutes
MAKES: 10 twists

Shortening or cooking spray
  2 **large egg yolks**
  1 **tablespoon water**
  ⅓ **cup granulated sugar**
  ½ **teaspoon ground cinnamon**
  ½ **teaspoon ground cardamom**
  1 **(17.3-ounce) package frozen
     puff pastry sheets, thawed**
  ½ **cup finely chopped roasted
     pistachio nuts**
  2 **tablespoons butter, melted**

1. Preheat the oven to 400°F. Lightly grease 2 baking sheets with shortening or cooking spray. Beat the egg yolks and 1 tablespoon water with a wire whisk in a small bowl. Stir together the sugar, cinnamon, and cardamom in a separate small bowl.

2. Place the puff pastry on a lightly floured surface. Carefully roll each sheet of puff pastry into a 9½-inch square. Brush each sheet with the egg mixture; sprinkle with 2 tablespoons sugar mixture. Sprinkle nuts evenly over 1 sheet, leaving a ¼-inch border; top with the remaining sheet, sugared side down. Firmly press edges to seal. Brush the top of the pastry with melted butter; sprinkle with the remaining sugar mixture.

3. Using a pizza cutter, cut pastry into ¾-inch strips. Twist each strip 3 times; place 2 inches apart on the prepared baking sheets.

4. Bake at 400°F for 19 minutes or until golden. Immediately transfer to wire racks. Serve warm or cool.

SUGARY CHOCOLATE-CHERRY SHORTBREAD

HANDS-ON: 20 minutes
TOTAL: 1 hour, 30 minutes
MAKES: about 5 dozen cookies

Aluminum foil

Shortening

- ½ **cup plus 1 tablespoon granulated sugar**
- 8 **ounces (1 cup) butter, softened**
- ½ **cup powdered sugar**
- 2½ **cups (11.25 ounces) all-purpose flour**
- ⅛ **teaspoon salt**
- ¼ **cup miniature semisweet chocolate chips**
- ¼ **cup finely chopped dried cherries**
- 1 **teaspoon vanilla extract**

1. Preheat the oven to 325°F. Line an 8-inch square pan with the aluminum foil, leaving foil overhanging at 2 opposite sides of the pan. Grease the foil with shortening; sprinkle with 1 tablespoon granulated sugar.

2. Put the butter in a large bowl. Beat with an electric mixer at medium speed until creamy; add the powdered sugar, beating well. Stir together the flour and salt in a medium bowl; gradually add to the butter mixture, beating until well blended. Stir in the chocolate chips, cherries, and vanilla. Press the dough into the prepared pan.

3. Bake at 325°F for 40 minutes or until golden. Cool in the pan 30 minutes or until slightly warm. Lift the shortbread from the pan, using the foil sides as handles. Gently remove the foil. With a sharp knife, cut into 8 rows by 8 rows. Dip the shortbread squares in the remaining granulated sugar.

CORNMEAL-PECAN SHORTBREAD

HANDS-ON: 1 hour, 30 minutes
TOTAL: 2 hours
MAKES: 42 shortbread cookies

Parchment paper

- 10 ounces (½ cup plus 6 tablespoons) butter, softened
- 2 cups finely shredded Parmesan cheese (8 ounces)
- 1 teaspoon salt
- ¼ teaspoon cayenne pepper
- ½ cup stone-ground yellow cornmeal
- ½ cup finely chopped pecans
- 1½ cups (6.75 ounces) all-purpose flour

TIP: Balance the sweetness of the holidays with this savory snack. Serve these yummy crackers with marinated olives and a selection of gourmet meats and cheeses.

1. Preheat the oven to 350°F. Line baking sheets with the parchment paper.

2. Put the butter, cheese, salt, and cayenne pepper in a large bowl. Beat with an electric mixer at medium speed 2 minutes or until well blended. Add the cornmeal and pecans; beat just until blended. Gradually add the flour, beating at low speed until blended. (The dough will be crumbly, yet moist enough to cling together when pressed.)

3. Turn out dough onto parchment paper and roll to ¼-inch thickness. Roll the dough to ¼-inch thickness on the parchment paper. Cut with a 2-inch round cutter, gently pressing together and rerolling the dough scraps as necessary. Place the cutouts 1 inch apart on the prepared baking sheets.

4. Bake at 350°F for 15 to 17 minutes or until light golden brown and crisp. Transfer to wire racks. Cool completely.

BUTTERSCOTCH-PECAN FUDGE

HANDS-ON: 35 minutes
TOTAL: 2 hours, 35 minutes
MAKES: 4 dozen pieces

Butter
- 1½ cups packed dark brown sugar
- 4 ounces (½ cup) butter
- 1 (5-ounce) can evaporated milk
- 1 (7-ounce) jar marshmallow creme
- 1 (11-ounce) bag butterscotch chips
- 1 cup chopped pecans

1. Grease the bottom and sides of an 8-inch square pan with butter. Put the brown sugar, ½ cup butter, and milk in a 3-quart heavy saucepan, and cook over medium heat, stirring constantly, until the butter is melted.

2. Stir in the marshmallow creme. Heat to boiling over medium heat; boil about 5 minutes, stirring occasionally, to 234°F on a candy thermometer or until a small amount of the mixture dropped into a cup of very cold water forms a soft ball that flattens when removed from the water; remove from heat. Add the butterscotch chips; stir until smooth. Stir in the pecans.

3. Spread fudge in the prepared pan. Let stand 2 hours or until firm. Cut into 6 rows by 8 rows.

White Chocolate
kies 'N Cream
Fudge

WHITE CHOCOLATE COOKIES 'N' CREAM FUDGE

HANDS-ON: 15 minutes
TOTAL: 1 hour, 15 minutes
MAKES: 4 pounds fudge

Butter

Aluminum foil

- 1 cup granulated sugar
- 6 ounces (¾ cup) butter
- 1 (5-ounce) can evaporated milk
- 2 (12-ounce) packages white chocolate chips
- 1 (7-ounce) jar marshmallow creme
- 3 cups coarsely crushed cream-filled chocolate sandwich cookies (about 25 cookies)

Pinch of salt

TIP: This is definitely a kid-favorite recipe! It's perfect for any school holiday party.

1. Grease a 9-inch square pan with butter. Line with the aluminum foil.

2. Stir together the sugar, butter, and milk in a medium saucepan. Cook over medium-high heat, stirring constantly, until mixture comes to a boil; cook 3 minutes, stirring constantly. Remove from the heat; add the white chocolate chips, marshmallow creme, 2 cups of the crushed cookies, and salt. Stir until the chips melt.

3. Pour the fudge into the prepared pan. Sprinkle the remaining 1 cup of the cookies over the fudge, gently pressing the cookies into the fudge. Cover and chill until firm (1 to 2 hours).

4. Lift the fudge from the pan, using the foil sides as handles. Gently remove the foil. Cut the fudge into squares.

WHITE PEANUT BUTTER FUDGE BARS

HANDS-ON: 10 minutes
TOTAL: 1 hour, 10 minutes
MAKES: 3 dozen bars

Aluminum foil

- 4 cups powdered sugar
- 1 cup chunky peanut butter
- 8 ounces (1 cup) butter, melted
- ⅔ cup graham cracker crumbs (10 squares)
- 8 ounces white chocolate, chopped
- ⅓ cup chopped peanuts

1. Line the bottom and sides of a 9-inch square pan with the aluminum foil, allowing 2 to 3 inches to extend over the sides. Stir together the powdered sugar, peanut butter, butter, and graham cracker crumbs until well blended. Press into bottom of the prepared pan.

2. Put the white chocolate in a medium-size microwave-safe bowl; microwave, uncovered, at HIGH 1 to 2 minutes or until melted and smooth, stirring at 30-second intervals. Pour the melted white chocolate over the peanut butter mixture, and spread to the edges. Sprinkle with the peanuts. Chill 1 hour or until the chocolate is set. Lift the fudge from the pan, using the foil sides as handles. Gently remove the foil. Cut into 6 rows by 6 rows.

CHOCOLATE GRANOLA BRITTLE

HANDS-ON: 20 minutes
TOTAL: 40 minutes
MAKES: 1 pound brittle

Cooking spray

- 1 cup granulated sugar
- ½ cup light corn syrup

Dash of salt

- 1 cup coarsely chopped pecans
- 1 tablespoon butter
- 1 teaspoon vanilla extract
- 1 teaspoon baking soda

Parchment paper

- ¾ cup chocolate granola
- 3 ounces semisweet chocolate, chopped
- 1½ tablespoons shortening

1. Lightly coat a rimless baking sheet with the cooking spray. Put the sugar, corn syrup, and dash of salt in a 2-quart microwave-safe glass bowl; microwave at HIGH 5 minutes. Stir in the pecans. Microwave 1½ minutes. Stir in the butter and vanilla. Microwave 1 minute and 45 seconds or until the candy is the color of peanut butter. Stir in the baking soda. (The mixture will bubble.)

2. Quickly pour the candy onto the prepared baking sheet. (Pour as thinly as possible without spreading the candy.) Cover the brittle quickly with the parchment paper, and use a rolling pin to thin out the candy; peel off the parchment paper. Sprinkle the granola over the brittle. Replace parchment paper, and use the rolling pin to adhere the granola to the brittle; peel off the parchment paper. Cool the brittle completely; break into desired-size pieces.

3. Put the semisweet chocolate squares and shortening in a small microwave-safe bowl; microwave at HIGH 1½ to 2 minutes, stirring after 1 minute. Dip each piece of brittle halfway into the chocolate mixture. Place the dipped brittle on the parchment paper to harden. Store in an airtight container at room temperature.

MILK CHOCOLATE–PEANUT BUTTER BARK

HANDS-ON: 10 minutes
TOTAL: 40 minutes
MAKES: 16 pieces

Aluminum foil

1 **cup milk chocolate chips**

1 **cup peanut butter chips**

½ **cup chopped salted peanuts**

1. Line a baking sheet with the aluminum foil. Melt the chocolate chips and peanut butter chips in a 2-quart saucepan over low heat, stirring constantly until smooth. Remove from heat. Stir in the peanuts.

2. Spread the mixture to ¼-inch thickness on the prepared baking sheet. Chill about 30 minutes or until set. Break into pieces.

MAKE

For a pretty presentation, place several pieces of the bark in a foil baking cup, and place on a cookie plate with other holiday treats.

METRIC EQUIVALENTS

The information in the following charts is provided to help cooks outside the United States successfully use the recipes in this book. All equivalents are approximate.

COOKING/OVEN TEMPERATURES

	Fahrenheit	Celsius	Gas Mark
Freeze Water	32° F	0° C	
Room Temp.	68° F	20° C	
Boil Water	212° F	100° C	
Bake	325° F	160° C	3
	350° F	180° C	4
	375° F	190° C	5
	400° F	200° C	6
	425° F	220° C	7
	450° F	230° C	8
Broil			Grill

LIQUID INGREDIENTS BY VOLUME

¼ tsp	=					1 ml
½ tsp	=					2 ml
1 tsp	=					5 ml
3 tsp	=	1 Tbsp	=	½ fl oz	=	15 ml
2 Tbsp	=	⅛ cup	=	1 fl oz	=	30 ml
4 Tbsp	=	¼ cup	=	2 fl oz	=	60 ml
5⅓ Tbsp	=	⅓ cup	=	3 fl oz	=	80 ml
8 Tbsp	=	½ cup	=	4 fl oz	=	120 ml
10⅔ Tbsp	=	⅔ cup	=	5 fl oz	=	160 ml
12 Tbsp	=	¾ cup	=	6 fl oz	=	180 ml
16 Tbsp	=	1 cup	=	8 fl oz	=	240 ml
1 pt	=	2 cups	=	16 fl oz	=	480 ml
1 qt	=	4 cups	=	32 fl oz	=	960 ml
				33 fl oz	=	1000 ml = 1 l

DRY INGREDIENTS BY WEIGHT
(To convert ounces to grams, multiply the number of ounces by 30.)

1 oz	=	⅟₁₆ lb	=	30 g
4 oz	=	¼ lb	=	120 g
8 oz	=	½ lb	=	240 g
12 oz	=	¾ lb	=	360 g
16 oz	=	1 lb	=	480 g

LENGTH
(To convert inches to centimeters, multiply the number of inches by 2.5.)

1 in	=			2.5 cm
6 in	=	½ ft	=	15 cm
12 in	=	1 ft	=	30 cm
36 in	=	3 ft = 1 yd	=	90 cm
40 in	=			100 cm = 1 m

EQUIVALENTS FOR DIFFERENT TYPES OF INGREDIENTS

Standard Cup	Fine Powder (ex. flour)	Grain (ex. rice)	Granular (ex. sugar)	Liquid Solids (ex. butter)	Liquid (ex. milk)
1	140 g	150 g	190 g	200 g	240 ml
¾	105 g	113 g	143 g	150 g	180 ml
⅔	93 g	100 g	125 g	133 g	160 ml
½	70 g	75 g	95 g	100 g	120 ml
⅓	47 g	50 g	63 g	67 g	80 ml
¼	35 g	38 g	48 g	50 g	60 ml
⅛	18 g	19 g	24 g	25 g	30 ml

INDEX

A

Almonds

B

Bars. *See also* **Brownies; Cookies and Bars.**
Brownies

C

Cakes
Candy. *See also* **Fudge.**

Chocolate